You Are Me

Danny James

PAGE PUBLISHING, INC.
Conneaut Lake, PA

First originally published by Page Publishing 2021

ISBN 978-1-6624-4817-1 (pbk)
ISBN 978-1-6624-4819-5 (hc)
ISBN 978-1-6624-4818-8 (digital)

Printed in the United States of America

Part 1

CHAPTER 1
When Your Day Comes

My child, this story is for you who is hurting inside. You have no one who can possibly understand what happened to you and what it did to your soul. The real cruelty of life's events is so unfair that you give up even trying to pretend that you care. Soul-crushing indignity and pain make you question your existence. I know who you are... because you are *me*.

You are never ready for when your life changes in a most devastating fashion. In an instant, everything that was is now gone. Everything that you held dear is gone. Everything that you loved about yourself is gone, and everything that you hoped for is gone. There is nothing left of your life that was. Nothing, and I truly mean *nothing*, is ever going to be the same again. And there is nothing you can do to stop or change it.

I understand that everyone has that event, that day, that *thing* that changes their entire life for the worse. Everyone can look back on that worst day of their life. There's no doubt about that. Not everyone, however, has had to endure a soul-wrecking tragedy that makes a person question if there is a God. The question then becomes: if there is a God, why would God let this happen to *me*? The thoughts should never have to cross your mind, but some circumstances call for it. When it does happen to you, you question whether you can ever truly recover from that event and ever be happy again.

After that "thing" that happened, people aren't the same, your day-to-day isn't the same, and *you* aren't the same. Some people will no longer choose to be in your life because of what happened to you.

It's not your fault; they simply can't be constantly reminded that the next horrible thing could happen to them. They can't continue to look at you and wonder, *What if that were me?* It's simply too much for them.

You won't continue to want some people in your life either. Many people won't fathom how you feel, which is almost worse than the event itself. Having someone say, "It's not that bad," or "It's going to be okay," is *not* what you want to hear or what you need to hear. Those are niceties that people say to minimize the gravity and reality of what really happened. It's condescending and unwanted. Feeling like *no one* can truly understand how you feel, what you endured, and what you went through is a most awful feeling. Your life is demarcated forever as "before the event" and "after the event."

For me, I will say that the story I am about to tell you is about a tragedy as bad as a person can endure. Unfortunately, I have had several of these terrible, horrible events, and there is a demarcation in my life for each—life before the event and life after the event.

I do want to note that there is a flip side to this condition as well. There are those momentously amazing events that mark a before-life and after-life event too. I have also experienced some of the most wonderous events a person is lucky enough to have. In your life, though you may have many of these amazing events and awful events, there are probably one, two, or maybe three that surpass all others. These are epoch changers versus chapter changers. My most awful event would start an epoch of agony and suffering that I would never wish upon anyone.

My most unfathomable event happened on an unsuspecting spring day in Omaha, Nebraska, in 1995. I was twenty-seven years old and planning to attend my ten-year high school reunion in just a few months. My family had moved from a farm in Minnesota to a small town north of Anchorage, Alaska, when I was in the middle of eleventh grade. So I had two high school reunions I wanted to attend. I had recently moved to Omaha with my boyfriend, Stuart. We met four years earlier when I attended my cousin's wedding in Omaha. I had gone to a nightclub the day after the wedding and met Stuart there. We fell in love that night, and we decided that he would move from Omaha to Fairbanks, Alaska, while I finished graduate school. We were both young and adventurous.

Shortly after moving to Omaha, we moved into a middle-class, nicely decorated home on a boulevard across from a Catholic cathedral with our five dogs and three cats. I worked at a telemarketing company that took orders for people who called a 1-800 number after seeing a commercial or infomercial on television. I was responsible for quality control statistics. Life was nice in Omaha, and Stuart and I had many friends. He was in community theater, which came with a built-in group of friends who loved to get together and entertain. We were happy.

Stuart's dad lived right outside Omaha, Nebraska, in Red Oak, Iowa, and would come over on occasion for dinner. I would make a baked chicken, broccoli-rice casserole, and a homemade fruit pie. His dad was a former minister for a church. He loved his son, and I believe he loved me too. He also loved homemade pie. Stuart's mother had died a few months before I met him, and throughout her life with her husband, she would make a homemade pie each week. Memories and traditions are important and all that we have when someone leaves us. Making homemade pie for Stuart's father was my way of continuing a tradition that he loved. I wish I had been able to meet Stuart's mom.

I thought I was living the life I had always wanted and always dreamed of having. The sneaky thing about these unfathomable events is that there is no warning. You could be going about your day, and then that's it. Every morning I would wake up to the same routine. I would make coffee, let our five little dogs go outside in our backyard, have some oatmeal, shower, dress, get in the car, and drive to work. Same thing every day. And I was fine with that.

The drive to work was only fifteen minutes. I would take US Interstate Highway 80 most of the way. I remember that we were having a false spring day. It was seventy degrees and sunshine in Omaha. There were lots of small, puffy clouds in the sky that day. Omaha is very flat, and it feels like you can see for a thousand miles in every direction when you stand still and take the time to look. I drove a Toyota-something, a small, unassuming two-door gray car. Along the route to work was a turn and a dip on the interstate. This day, as I came upon the turn and the dip, there was traffic, and I had to stop.

There had been nothing particularly noteworthy about the day so far. Nothing to give me any indication of what was going to happen…until now. Now, time suddenly stood still while I sat in my plain gray car with my pressed shirt just waiting for traffic to move. Now is where my life and my world would change forever. Now is when you wish you had done all those things on your bucket list— those things you always put off for later. Now is that moment when your life comes into focus of what is truly important, but it's too late. You waited too long to realize what was important, to act on your dreams and your aspirations.

This moment seemed to take minutes, but I know realistically it was a fraction of a second. I distinctly remember the sun being warm on my skin. It was a beautiful day. I had the window open, so I could feel the warm breeze and breath in the fresh air. I could hear a flock of Canadian geese honking in the sky, flying North for the summer. I hadn't really woken up yet, and I was very casually going about my day. I had ironed a shirt to go with my gray suit coat and slacks— plain, boring, safe. Then it happened. That moment you never want to have happen. That thing you can't think of too much because you wouldn't be able to get out of bed each day. I instinctively glanced in the rearview mirror to see a blue pickup truck coming toward my car at full speed. The man in the truck must not have seen that traffic was backed up.

Again, this was only a matter of a second, but it sticks in my memory like a full-length feature movie. Right before I saw the truck smash into my rear bumper, I let out a primal scream and started to weep. The truck was coming at me way too fast, and I knew at that very moment that I was going to die in this car accident. I didn't want to die. It is ironic how when you are facing death, everything about your life becomes so clear. In my mind flashed a memory of my mom bringing out my birthday cake on my sixth birthday. Another flash: my Arabian filly, Abigail, and I riding across a freshly cut field of hay when I was in tenth grade. And another: I saw my brother, Wayne, when he was a baby in his high chair eating SpaghettiOs. So many memories flooded my mind, and I wept. I knew this was my last moment alive, and I bawled, "Noooo!" I would never see my friends and family again. This can't be how my story ends.

I saw the face of the man driving the blue truck. He was in his thirties with black hair and a mustache. I don't think he ever saw my car, as he was looking down in his lap as if he had spilled something. The blue truck's bumper crushed the plastic covering of my rear bumper. I could hear the explosive crash as the truck thrust into my bumper. A wave of crushing force hurled my body, first back into the seat and headrest and then forward, smashing my head into the windshield. The broken pieces of my car shattered like a drinking glass that had been dropped on the kitchen floor.

I was wearing a seat belt, but I propelled forward into the windshield as if I wasn't. As my head smashed into the windshield, my car jumped forward and hit the car in front of mine. The noise of the crash was deafening, then complete and utter silence as everything stopped. I was knocked unconscious. I was alive but I was soon to find out that my life was over.

CHAPTER 2
The Day After the End

The next day, it wasn't immediately apparent that anything had changed besides the fact that my rear bumper was now in the back seat of my car. There are things you don't realize about a most awful event while it is happening to you. Perhaps you don't want to believe that anything is different, that anything has changed. You don't want to see that anything is wrong. Denial is a powerful thing, isn't it? I didn't want to believe that anything was wrong, but it was. Something was *terribly* wrong, and I was terrified to admit it. I was even more afraid to see it. If I didn't see it as real, maybe it wasn't real.

I told Stuart that I wanted to go to work. I had a bad headache, but I really wanted to put all this behind me. Stuart told me to stay home in bed and take it easy. He would be back after work and check in on me. I had gotten myself dressed for work but apparently had some issues. I had put my pants on over my pajamas and had put on one sandal and one dress shoe. Strange, but I didn't think too deeply about it. I was tired, anyway, so I agreed to stay home. Except for the bump on my forehead, I looked normal.

I tried to make myself a cup of coffee but was clumsy and had difficulty picking things up and holding them. I had dropped and broken my coffee mug and spilled grounds all over the counter. My hands felt like they weren't working right. My body ached, and my head ached even more. I definitely had some whiplash. Throughout the morning, I felt disoriented and confused. I had to hang on to the handrail on the stairway that led to our bedroom upstairs just to get up the steps. That was a first since moving into the house. I was having difficulty remembering words and names, and I was very tired. Something seemed very wrong, but I couldn't understand what. I knew I certainly had PTSD from my near-death experience the day before and that I was extremely angry with the man who smashed into my car. I kept envisioning the truck racing at me, the driver oblivious to everything going on.

Throughout the morning, I felt like I was zoning out for minutes at a time. I was starting to get frustrated at my inability to think clearly. I sat down on the floor of my hallway, trying to figure out what was happening to me. I felt fear, anger, and frustration. I was afraid I was losing my mind.

I looked in the mirror hanging in the hall, and I didn't look as damaged as I felt I should. I had to tell someone, anyone, what was happening.

"I need help, please, someone help me," I repeated over and over in a monotone voice, but there was no one to hear me. Stuart had gone to work, and I was alone in the big house on Fontenelle Boulevard. Tears started slowly dripping from my eyes. I could feel each drop trickle down my cheek. How could anyone else understand what was happening to me if I couldn't understand what was happening? I was afraid that no one would believe something was wrong with me. After all, I *looked* fine. I had to do something. I was panicking. I needed someone, *anyone*, to help me. I needed someone to believe me that something was wrong.

As I sat in the hallway, I gazed in the mirror at my reflection. My bruised head didn't seem bruised enough. *If I look more damaged, then someone would know I needed help*, I thought. S I smashed my forehead into the wall where I had been sitting for the last several hours. *Bang. Bang.* The pain of my face hitting the wall swelled my eyes with tears. The pain was real and helped distract me from what was going on in my head. I smashed my forehead into the rose-patterned wallpaper again and again.

There is something wrong, so very wrong, I thought. *Bang. Bang.* The tears began to pour from my eyes like a thunderstorm on a car's windshield. I could hardly see, but I kept going. I braced my hands on the wall, planted my feet firmly, and hit my head in rapid succession. "What the hell is wrong with me!" I screamed at the top of my lungs. *Bam, bam, bam.* I struck my head again and again. *Something is so wrong*, I said to myself. I looked in the mirror, and my outside still didn't look as bad as I knew my insides were. My eyes were swollen and red with tears. My eyes burned and stung. My nose ran with snot from crying. I could smell burning tires, but there was no fire. Then everything smelled like rotting garbage, but there was no garbage. It was an awful, pungent smell.

"What the hell is wrong with me!" I yelled at the universe.

I stopped banging my head on the wall and just sat staring at the damaged wallpaper for a while. I then walked down the steps from the hallway to the kitchen, holding the walls as I went down each step as if I was trying to hold up my world. We kept our five little dogs in the kitchen, and when I stepped in, they all started jumping on my legs. My legs felt weak, and I couldn't stay standing. Slowly, I fell on my knees and then to the floor. Something was wrong, and I couldn't understand what. The little dogs piled on me as I lay on the cold tile. *They* could tell something was wrong; dogs always know when something is wrong.

I got back up on my knees and then on my feet. My legs were wobbly, and my head felt like a cloud of confusion. I opened the fridge and saw my car keys and wallet were in the deli drawer. Did I put them there? Did Stuart? Did he try to hide my car keys? Nothing was making sense. Nothing was where it was supposed to be. I wanted a glass of milk but could not find the milk. I know we had some, but it was nowhere in sight.

I suddenly felt like I could fall asleep at any moment and needed to lie down. I looked around the walls and counters and cabinets, searching for the way out of the kitchen. I needed to lie down. I needed to get to my bedroom. I just needed to lie down. I started frantically opening cabinet doors as if these were doors out of the kitchen. I opened the fridge door, but that was not the way out of the kitchen either. Panic-stricken, I patted my hands all along the walls; there had to be a way out. *Pat, pat, pat.* There has to be a way out of here. I patted my hands on the counters, the cabinets, the walls. What was happening to me?! Why can't I find the door? I was getting frustrated and so very tired.

I couldn't figure out how to get back to my bedroom. There were walls in the kitchen, but I couldn't figure out how to get out. I was trapped in the kitchen. I couldn't find the door. I lay on the wood floor with all the bits of dog hair and scraps of dog food. I was breathing very quickly, and my heart was racing. My nose was still running, and my eyes stung from the tears. My dog, Bobo, licked my eyes and snuffled his nose at me. Each of the little dogs took their turn, licking my face, and then piled on me to comfort me. Somehow, I fell asleep.

I don't know how long I had been on the floor when Stuart came home from work. I heard him come through the front door, call to me, and go up the stairs to our bedroom. I tried to yell to him, but no words would come out of my mouth. I needed to tell him what was happening to me. He would know what to do. I needed him to understand and help me. I needed him more than I have ever needed someone. *I'm here in the kitchen, please find me*, I was saying silently to him.

Then Stuart opened the door to the kitchen. Our five little dogs ran over to him. I was lying on the floor on my back, contorted. He looked at me, and I could see fear and sadness on his face. He said no words. He was stunned. All that would come from my mouth was a jumbled mess of words that made no sense. "Stu-uu-rt, sum ting is wong me," I mumbled, and a glob of spit drooled down the corner of my mouth to the floor. I looked up at him from the floor, tears dripping out of my eyes, hoping he understood. I *needed* him to understand that something was wrong. Could he understand me? I was so confused and overwhelmed that all I could do was weep. My hands wouldn't move like I wanted them to move. My legs wouldn't hold me up. My mouth wouldn't make the right sounds.

That morning, I had been confused with aches and pains, and I was somewhat disoriented. By that evening, I was struggling to speak and walk. Over the next few days, I completely lost my ability to talk and understand Stuart when he spoke. I lost my ability to walk and resorted to crawling to get to the bathroom.

With each hour that passed, I lost memories of another friend and another family member. Stuart, the love of my life, was the last person I could recognize. Eventually, I could no longer remember him either. As I lay in bed, Stuart leaned over and kissed my forehead. For a second, I knew it was him, and then nothing. I looked at him blankly as if he was a stranger. I was now alone in the world in my head. With each passing moment, I lost memories and knowledge until there was nothing left but darkness.

I had seen the fear in Stuart's face as he saw me lying on the kitchen floor. He couldn't have foreseen the sadness that was to come upon our home, but he could see that I was no longer the person he met and fell in love with four years earlier. I was now crippled and handicapped. He was no longer the person I fell in love with either. To me, Stuart was now a complete stranger.

*****

For the next two years, I lay in my bed and slept for twenty-two hours a day. When I was awake, I knew nothing. I remembered nothing of my life before the car accident—not my family, not my friends, nothing about my former life. Everything was gone as if my life had never happened. I could not remember things that happened moments ago, much less earlier that day or the prior year. I had no understanding of how to do simple tasks like brushing teeth or tying a shoelace. Everything that I learned to do throughout my entire life was erased from my brain.

Little did I know, knowing nothing was much better than what was to come. Sometimes knowing nothing is comfortable. It is not painful. There is no pain or loss in knowing *nothing*. You don't know what you don't know, and sometimes that is the best you can hope for.

What I didn't know is that I had ripped the neurons in my brain when my forehead hit the windshield of my car. Over the three days since the accident, the last bits of neurotransmitters were being used up by my brain. My brain could no longer process information.

There was no "me" left after the collision with the blue truck on Interstate 80 that warm spring day in April. Everything was gone.

CHAPTER 3
The Three Jeans

This isn't funny now, but we would joke about the crazy relative that some family in town had locked up in their attic when I was growing up. I was now that crazy person locked in the attic. I would lie in bed and look out the second-story window at people in the street. I didn't know how to get out of the bedroom. Stuart only had to shut the door; I simply didn't understand the concept of a door. Stuart would take me to doctor's appointments, but that was the only time I would leave the room. At night, he would lie with me. I had no understanding of what was happening, who he was, or who I was. I don't remember speaking to him during those two years because I don't think I could understand speech very well.

I know during this time that Stuart had to be going through his own difficulties. I had lost my job, lost my income, lost my memory, and lost all my abilities to care for myself. Stuart had become a full-time caretaker for someone who didn't even recognize him. Looking back, I don't understand how I was left in that room for two years. Were there other options? Did anyone visit me? While I have almost no memory of what happened during those two years, there are brief snips.

I know there were birds, lovebirds and cockatiels, I believe. Stuart had wanted me to have company while he was away during the day, so he bought several caged birds. I would usually be awake for a few hours when the sun was at its peak. My bed lay next to the window on the second floor of our house. The sun would feel warm as I lay there, barely conscious of what was around me. When the sun was at its warmest, the birds would all start to chatter and flap their wings.

Each day, the birds would quiet down after some time, and I would go back to sleep for another day. I later found that Stuart had bought over eighty caged birds to keep me company. Why were there so many birds? I still wonder about that.

After two years with brain damage and complete amnesia, I eventually learned, or rather I remembered, how to walk better. I could speak well enough for people to understand me. When Stuart would take me places, I would usually wait in his truck and sleep. I was sleeping twelve to eighteen hours a day and beginning to understand what had happened and what I had lost. I had thought I was pretty smart when I was growing up. I did well in school; I was my small town's high school valedictorian and then went to college and graduate school. I recall my grandpa always saying, "They can take everything from you, but they can't take your education." I remember now how proud he was when I graduated with my master's degree in math from the University of Alaska. I was the first of his grandchildren to graduate from college, much less graduate school.

As I awoke from spending two years in a semicoma, I slowly realized what had happened and what I had lost. There is no politically correct way to say this, but I was now severely, mentally retarded. I was both physically and mentally disabled. I was a simpleton. I struggled to put words into sentences. I couldn't read. I wasn't able to take care of myself very well. It was as if I was a baby all over again, having to relearn to read and talk. I had to relearn how to walk and navigate the world, except I was now thirty years old. I look back and wonder how people perceived me during the limited times I would go out of the house to doctors' appointments. I have no idea. Did anyone know who I was before all of this? Did anyone know I was normal before, that I had a job and friends and all the things a normal person has? Could they see that this was from an accident? Or maybe they just assumed I was born this way. After all, it's so much easier to see a handicapped person and feel sorry for their lot in life rather than believe that it could ever happen to them.

I walked very stiltedly, and I had an uncontrollable jerk and made random loud noises. The doctors called it a myoclonic seizure disorder. It looked just like Tourette's syndrome. I could usually feel it coming on. It would start with my eyes rolling back in my head, my face would jerk, and a loud grunt or bark would come from my mouth. This could happen dozens and dozens of times a day. As if being handicapped wasn't bad enough, I had a disorder that drew attention to my having a disability. I never got used to the jerks and grunts; I was always self-conscious.

When you don't know what you don't know, you can be okay with everything. The horror of it all comes when you find out what you don't know and what you don't have anymore. Then the resentfulness, bitterness, and anger set in. The unfairness of life pervades every thought of every day. *Why did I get hit by a car? Was it bad karma? Had I done something to deserve this lot in life?* The more I thought about what I had lost, the sadder and more desperate I became.

I had probably been crying for several days straight when Stuart brought me to a mental hospital for the first time. I stayed at Nebraska Medical Health Center for a week to be evaluated. While I was there, I met three patients who all had the same name—at least, I *think* they all had the same name. I called them all Jean—Jean 1, a very large older woman who had lost her senior mother; Jean 2, a big-breasted woman who had brain damage like me; and Jean 3, a nurse with Crohn's disease who had become addicted to pain medication.

All four of us would have therapy sessions and discuss why we were in the mental hospital. Jean 1 would repeatedly state that she didn't know why she was even at the mental hospital. Her husband had checked her in. Jean 1's mom was her best friend her entire life, and her mom had recently passed away after a few years of fighting some kind of cancer. Apparently, Jean 1 took a bottle of sleeping pills after not being able to cope with her mom dying. "I'm fine," Jean 1 would say. "I should be home. I don't even know why I'm here." She was always smiling behind tears and would talk about how much she loved her mom and missed her.

Jean 2 was probably a very popular woman before she was in a car accident that caused her brain damage. She was thin with curvy hips, very large breasts, and long wavy black hair. Her feet and knees pointed at each other, and she had to rock back and forth to walk. Her left arm was bent at the elbow, stuck forever with her hand waving goodbye. She had a beautiful face but couldn't move the left side. Jean 2 was pissed at the world. She was mad at her husband for not spending enough time with her, the guy who hit her fifteen years earlier, and the doctors for not giving her enough pain medication. 2 was seventeen when she was partying with her boyfriend and got into a car accident driving home. Her boyfriend died. Jean 2 ended up in a coma and then this—permanently disabled physically and mentally with no real working memory. Jean 2 took a lot of prescription medication, and her husband, whom she met after her accident, thought she needed to be reevaluated after she tried to stab him with a knife, so he brought her in.

Thinking about her had me asking myself all sorts of questions. Was I going to be like Jean 2, forever mentally and physically handicapped? Did I look like her, handicapped? Did people see me like I saw Jean 2, a crazy invalid with no real hope for happiness? How did she have a husband? What was he like? Why would someone ever want to be tied to a crazy invalid? I could only imagine…

Jean 3 was a nurse at the same hospital we were in. She had been diagnosed with Crohn's disease a few years earlier. She had had three surgeries for it and had several feet of intestines removed. As a result, she had a stoma on her belly with a bag for poop. Jean 3 had been caught stealing pain medication from her patients. She didn't think she had any problem. The missing medication at work was an "accident." She didn't have a problem with prescription medication. Right, Jean 3, no one believes you, not even me.

After a week with these people, I knew I wasn't anything like them. At least I didn't want to believe I was.

CHAPTER 4
Benevolence Society

As part of having a "disability" status for the social security administration and getting payments from the government, I was also able to get job training support. On paper, I looked like a good candidate for many jobs. I had worked for four years at an aerospace company teaching statistics and had a graduate degree in math. My physical disabilities had become less noticeable. I could now walk with a somewhat normal gait without the stiff, halting cautiousness I had for the last few years. I didn't drool much when I spoke, and I took medication for the jerking and grunting. I actually took a *lot* of medication.

The Benevolence Society, a nonprofit agency that helps handicapped people with job training, had found a job training opportunity for me with an engineering company. I'm not even sure what the job was. I put on a suit for my first day, and Stuart drove me to the company where I was met by my case manager from the Benevolence Society. I went in with my caseworker and sat down in the lobby. Several people came in and introduced themselves.

"Hello, nice to meet you!" I said enthusiastically to an older man in a suit. I met several other people and went around shaking hands and introducing myself. This was so weird, yet it seemed natural. Then after a very short period of time, my caseworker told me he would take me home. I wasn't exactly sure what was happening, but I was going along with the flow.

Sometimes when things seem too good to be real, they *are* too good to be real. My caseworker told me he was sorry but that this job training opportunity wasn't going to work out. I thought everything went well. I had on a nice suit. I didn't drool or jerk or bark while I was there. Still, as I was enthusiastically introducing myself to my new coworkers, I apparently introduced myself to the same people multiple times. I looked better on the outside but was still very broken on the inside. I couldn't remember who I had met from one moment to the next.

I knew it was too good to be real. I had gotten my hopes up, only to have them come crashing down. This was a pattern I would repeat over and over. I would get my hopes up, believing that something good was finally going to happen, only to have reality rear its ugly head. Then I would be disappointed and devastated and have to build up my courage to try again. It frankly seemed pointless.

I am very grateful for the support of the Benevolence Society. I had a few more attempts with them at getting a job. My memory was so poor at the time that I don't remember much. One job I do remember was for the Benevolence Society itself. I worked as the hands for a quadriplegic man named Mike, who was hit by a drunk driver in a car accident. The accident left his neck broken, and he was completely paralyzed from the neck down. There was a tube called a sip and puff switch that was set up as part of his wheelchair that he used to move. He would blow into the tube to make the chair function. He was my age with black hair and brown eyes, working as a computer engineer before his accident. He had a wife and two kids. We would sit at a desk together, and I would basically be his hands. He would tell me to insert disks, write things on labels, and type computer code lines on a computer keyboard.

Together, we could function as one person. Separately, we would die without the support of others. He would die of starvation, and I would die from something stupid, like sticking a fork in an electric socket. I don't know how this job ended, as it seemed like a good fit. Mike probably thought I was too stupid and asked for someone else to be his hands. I guess I'll never really know what happened…and I'm okay with that.

CHAPTER 5
Don't Trust Anyone

Stuart and I lived across from a Catholic cathedral. On Sundays, I would hear the bells chime, and our house was close enough that I could hear the congregation sing during Mass. Our neighbor across the street was a very old woman with her also old quadriplegic daughter. Every Sunday, I would see them both go down the sidewalk to attend Mass. The mother walked without a cane or walker, and the daughter had controls on her wheelchair like Mike did at the Benevolence Society. I later found that the mother was 104 and the daughter was 82. They always seemed happy.

I was desperately lonely and definitely not happy. I really wanted to meet them and find out how they could be so happy given their conditions. I started attending Mass each Sunday when my neighbor ladies did. They sat in the front row where a section of the pew had been moved to allow for a wheelchair. After Mass one Sunday, I decided to introduce myself as they sat waiting for everyone else to leave the church.

I walked up to the lady in the wheelchair and looked her square in her contorted face. "Hello, I'm your neighbor," I said proudly. "I live across the street from you."

"Nice to meet you," she said politely. "My name's Irene." Her speech was difficult to understand. Looking at her, she looked like any other grandma. She had wrinkly skin with short curly gray hair. Her face and body were contorted, with one side of her mouth pointing up and the other pointing down. Her arms were bent at the elbows and wrists in uncomfortable-looking positions, and her head was tilted to the right.

Shortly after I met Irene, her mother passed away. I came to find out Irene was born with severe multiple sclerosis. She had never been able to walk. She was born in Omaha, Nebraska, and had always lived in the same house. Her father lived into his late nineties, and her mother lived to be 104. People at church would later comment that the mother was driven to live so long to make sure her daughter was okay. In fact, everyone credited their long lives to the fact that they had a purpose. The purpose was to outlive their severely handicapped daughter to make sure she was always taken care of.

Despite being severely handicapped, Irene was happy and had many friends. Oddly enough, she had use of her toes on her right foot and was able to dial the telephone and talk to people. She could be propped up in a harness that allowed her to use her feet to type on a computer keyboard. Irene had online friends around the world. Since her mom died, she lived by herself in her house next to the cathedral. She had lived there all her eighty-two years.

Irene had twelve hours of care each day through an agency that provided a home health-care worker. She called me one morning and asked if I could help her for the day. Her morning worker called in sick, and the agency wasn't going to send anyone until six o'clock that evening to make her dinner and get her back into bed. Irene and I had bonded over being handicapped, so I told her I would. I walked across the street to her house and went in to find her lying in her bed, contorted, and with a strong smell of poop. I had only ever seen Irene clean, well dressed, and sitting in her highly mechanized wheelchair. She had a stoma, and it had come loose, hence the smell.

To see someone so helpless in such a deplorable state was shocking. I cleaned up the poop as best I could and helped Irene onto a wheelchair with a bedpan in it. Irene was used to getting up at six each morning, and it was now nine o'clock. So she had to pee. After peeing, I set Irene in her everyday wheelchair. She led me through the day's chores. I changed her bed linens and washed the dirty ones. Then I cleaned her bathroom and folded clean clothes from the dryer. Once that was done, I made her breakfast of oatmeal and yogurt and fed her. Remember, Irene had no control of her hands and arms. She could move her head and her toes, that was it, so feeding her was a bit of a challenge, to say the least. I made her a pot of coffee and poured a cup with milk and sugar. She was able to drink her coffee with a very long straw.

I was very tired from all the activities of the day, but I knew I needed to push through. I made Irene a lunch of fried romaine lettuce with yogurt. This was the routine all day. She would tell me what to do, and I would do it.

It made me feel good to be of use to someone. Over the next few weeks, Irene called me five or six more times to tell me that her worker had called in sick and she needed someone to take care of her daily chores. I would walk over to Irene's house, she would tell me step-by-step what to do, and I would do it. She was very patient and helped me figure out how to get everything done.

I liked Irene, and it felt like I had a friend who could accept me for who I was. I had no other handicapped friends and still spent most of my time sitting in my room with the lovebirds and cockatiels. It had been a few months since I stopped trying to work with the Benevolence Society. I don't think they realized how much help I needed when they signed up to help me.

*****

I am going to pause this story to say that when you have had a horrible thing happen to you, more awful things seem to follow. It's like the world *knows* you are a victim, and if anyone needs a victim, you will be there to raise your hand. You wear a sign on your forehead that reads, "Kick me because I'm already down, and no one will care." *No one* will fucking care, and that sucks.

*****

For about the sixth time in several weeks, Irene called early in the morning and asked me if I could help her with her chores. Her worker called in sick again, and the agency wasn't able to send anyone. I dutifully walked across the street and up to Irene's bedroom. She told me that she hadn't had a bath in a week and really needed me to give her one. I had dressed her, helped her on to her toilet, and changed her stoma, so I really didn't think this was going to be too bad.

I took out a large bath towel and laid it on Irene's bed. She told me to get a large pail with warm soapy water and a washrag. I followed her instructions to carefully remove her pajamas and lay her contorted body on the bed. I started with her face, neck, and ears, then rolled her to one side and washed her back and shoulders. I washed around her saggy, wrinkled breasts and back to the other side to wash her bottom like you would clean a baby's butt. Irene then directed me to wash between her legs. She said she felt dirty and needed me to scrub hard. I had the washcloth and was scrubbing as she directed me to scrub harder.

"I feel so dirty," she repeated over and over, so I scrubbed harder. Irene then moaned loudly and fell limp. I stopped and was worried that she had a heart attack. Quickly, I dried her off and got her dressed. She was smiling and wouldn't stop talking. *What had happened?* I thought to myself. I lifted Irene off the bed onto her wheelchair, and she still wouldn't shut up. *Why had she felt so dirty?* I wondered. She was acting so weird. I walked down the stairs to make her lunch of fried lettuce and yogurt. As I walked, I realized what had happened. She tricked me into getting her off. I dry-heaved in my mouth. *Gross!* I thought to myself. *How dare she do something like that!*

Irene had taken advantage of me, the retard on the block, and tricked me into sexually satisfying her. I was ashamed, embarrassed, and grossed out. I walked out the front door and never saw Irene again. She never called me again, so I know she knew what she was doing. I had thought we were friends. I thought there was some comradery between us handicapped people. No, I was so stupid that I was a joke to *other* handicapped people. Nice. I guess there is a hierarchy even with handicapped people. Those with only physical handicaps are over those of us with mental handicaps, I guess.

I could not figure out the motivations of others. This would come to haunt me over and over, as I was an easy target for people who wanted to take advantage of me for entertainment or their own personal gain. This was one aspect of being handicapped I never got used to. It's bad enough being handicapped, but then to have people either make fun of you for their entertainment? Or worse, to trick you for their personal gain? It was disgusting. Why do people take advantage of those who obviously can't defend themselves? Why? This isn't right, and it isn't okay. While handicapped, I was sexually exploited several times, and I had people steal from me. Why? What is wrong with some people? I wish I had an answer.

CHAPTER 6
Goober

I lost my will to try to get another job. After my last try at working with Mike at the Benevolence Society, I realized that not even the most desperate of employers would want me to work for them. I couldn't take getting rejected by another job, but I was not going to be discouraged. So I decided that maybe I could do something at home. The internet as we know it didn't exist at the time, so working at home for someone like me meant making something that I could sell for money. I needed to be able to do this by myself, with myself, for myself. Also, I really needed to find something to do with my time each day. I was handicapped but not lazy. Staying at home was very lonely, and I was afraid to go outside too much because I didn't want anyone to hurt me. Sounds a bit pathetic, I know, but I was learning to be afraid of everything. Afraid that other people would try to hurt me. Afraid I would never have another job. Afraid I would never be happy again.

I saw a documentary on PBS about a farmer in Pakistan who was raising angora rabbits for their wool. He would then have the wool spun into yarn, and then that yarn would get shipped around the world to be sold in yarn stores. *I could do that*, I thought and decided right there that I wanted to get an angora rabbit and learn how to spin its wool into yarn. I thought that maybe if I could do this, I could make and sell the yarn or maybe make mittens and sell them. I don't remember much about Stuart during the years he took care of me, but I do remember he did what he could to make me happy.

Stuart had gotten me four angora rabbit kits, and we set up cages for them in our basement. He bought a spinning wheel at an estate sale with a book on how to spin wool into yarn. The angora rabbits had long silky fur that shed out four times a year. It was so soft and fluffy, and I got excited just thinking about the possibilities. I really wanted to do this. These little bunnies were something that could give me some hope for working again and being able to support myself. I enjoyed brushing and grooming the rabbits and the daily chores of feeding them and cleaning their cages. Taking care of them gave me some purpose, some reason to get out of bed each day.

I sat down with the spinning book and opened the first page. *Fuck!* I thought to myself as I looked at the words. I forgot I didn't know how to read. Instead, I opened the spinning book and looked at the pictures. I knew the letters and their sounds, but each word was a struggle. I would figure out a word and then another, but by the time I got to the end of a sentence, I couldn't remember the words from the beginning. I kept trying because I really wanted to do this. I *needed* to do this. Each day I would open the spinning book and start from the first page. I could eventually get sentences but putting everything together was hard. My memory was still very poor, and by the time I got to each new sentence, the one before it was gone. Each day I would figure out another page, and I was beginning to remember what each sentence and each paragraph would say.

My rabbits were growing bigger, except one: Goober. When I got my rabbits, they were about eight weeks old and all from the same litter. Goober was the color of a wild rabbit, and his siblings were spotted with white and gray or white and brown. As the weeks passed, I realized something was wrong with Goober. His head and back feet were growing, but the rest of his body wasn't. After a few months, Goober's legs had walked their last steps, and he started dragging his back legs around his cage with his working front legs. I would guess that Goober had some form of rabbit cerebral palsy. He was happy, I was happy, and I guess that was enough. Goober was my handi-pet. He was basically a head with big ears, back legs, and a puffy tail. He could kind of push himself around his cage with his big back feet to get to his food dish and water bottle. Sometimes I would need to clean up his messy butt. He needed me to take care of him, and I needed him to give me some hope that life would get better. I think we all could use a little Goober in our lives sometimes.

CHAPTER 7
North to Alaska

Stuart had taken care of me for four years. Two years as a completely bedridden invalid and two more years as a simpleton who was always depressed. When he told me of his plan to send me back to live with my parents, I took a 22-shotgun my parents had sent for my birthday, pinned him to the floor, and threatened to shoot him. In retrospect, that was probably not the *best* way to get someone to keep you around; I was very damaged and hadn't really thought it through. A friend of Stuart's volunteered to drive my rabbits and me up North to live with my parents in Palmer, Alaska.

One thing to know about Alaskans is that their basic philosophy of life is, "You leave me alone, and I'll leave you alone." Simple. I arrived in Alaska at the end of summer. The tourists were all heading back to the Lower 48 in their cruise ships and RVs.

Stuart had split up our belongings and put my share in a rental truck. He gave me one of our cars, and my rabbits were in the car in small cages being towed behind the rental. Stuart had taught me the basics of driving again. I should not have had a driver's license, but I wasn't going to lose that too. Stuart's friend, Randy, drove us into Canada, over the Rocky Mountains, across the Yukon Territory, and into Alaska. I remember the song "Cryin'" playing on the radio as we crossed into the Yukon Territory.

"You're leaving and I'm cryin'," the radio belted out, and I realized I would never be with anyone again. Who would want to be with me? A retarded, fat, simpleton whom you can't take in public.

The song continued, "I'm cryin' but I'm stong enough to stop missing you, you'll be blue."

"No, *I'm* going to be blue," I said flatly to the radio. "And I know I'm not strong enough."

Goober died while we drove through the Yukon Territory. Any will I had to live died in the Yukon with Goober. I buried him along the side of the road in the cold tundra. Goober didn't want to go to Alaska, so he didn't. I dug my hands into a mound of cold sphagnum moss and made an opening big enough to fit in Goober's big head and legs. I covered the hole with the rest of the sphagnum moss. I didn't tell Randy that Goober had died. This was my rabbit and my dream that died. I didn't want anyone else to know.

There are some things that happen in your life that you can never, ever, ever tell anyone. You have reached the absolute bottom of your life. You have degraded yourself in so many ways for so long that there is no way to return from it. You can't face anyone who knew you before because they will obviously be able to see how defiled and degrading your existence has become. Most people have not had to hit some type of rock bottom to turn things around. My life in Omaha was heaven compared to what I was going to experience living in Alaska. While I want to be honest about my journey, I struggle with the absolute depravity that I put myself through while in Alaska. I have been in psychological therapy for years, and I've had friends that I've confided in. However, I have always been too ashamed to talk about most of the actual things that happened, the things I did while living as a handicapped, mental patient in Alaska. I have never told anyone what happened...until now.

CHAPTER 8
Employee of the Month

I kept trying to get a full-time job so I could have some sense of a future where I could support myself. Not knowing how, or if, you can support yourself is a very demoralizing feeling. I could count on my parents, but I didn't want to be dependent. My dad had colon cancer; what would happen if he died? I needed to have some veiled belief that I could support myself. I don't think I am very unique in this aspect. Not having a job is one thing, but not knowing if you can ever get and keep a job because you don't have any skills or abilities is completely different. I had worked a lot of odd jobs, but I couldn't keep any of them.

I kept trying different short-term jobs I got from temporary agencies in Anchorage. One time I delivered flowers on Mother's Day in Anchorage. The job paid minimum wage, but they lured you in by saying you could keep all your tips. No one tips a flower-delivery driver on Mother's Day. I shoveled snow and dirt from parking lots a couple of times. I ran background checks at the Anchorage Municipal Court House once a week for a company that did pre-employment background checks. I had a college degree, but that college degree didn't mean very much when I couldn't read very well and had trouble remembering what I was told to do at work. I was slow-moving and slow-thinking.

Then I got a temporary job working in an insurance company filing paperwork. It was the middle of winter in Anchorage, and there was one hour of daylight each day. The arctic sun would start to climb over the Chugach Mountains at about one o'clock each afternoon. Then just an hour later, after barely peeking over the horizon, it would sink into the Gulf of Alaska by two. The job I got involved filing insurance papers in a basement with racks and racks of file hangers. There was a sixteen-digit number on each file. Every so often, a basket would come down full of files that needed to be refiled, or a basket would come down with a list of files that needed to be pulled. I was told that if I did well as a temporary worker, there was an opportunity to get a full-time job that paid better, working upstairs. I could answer phone calls, fill out paperwork, and talk to customers. That seemed like a great job and a great opportunity.

When I arrived in the office building's arctic entry on my first day of work, there was a glass wall that separated the main part of the office from a stairway to the basement, where the file room was. On the other side of the glass, about fifty people sat at desks in front of computers, many talking on telephones. They looked like they had all been working together for a while. Many looked like they were friends, sitting and talking with coffee cups in their hands. I wanted what they had so badly, and I got lost staring at them—these people sitting at their desks with their telephones and coffee cups. I was just happy to *have* a job. I didn't care if the job didn't pay very much. I didn't care if the work was boring. To have coworkers whom you can look forward to seeing every day was a dream to me.

I really wanted to get this job. This was the first hope I had in forever. *I can answer phones and fill out forms and drink coffee*, I told myself. I really needed some hope. I tried to manifest the positive thoughts even harder. *Please just let me believe for a little while that this job can work out*, I thought. *That I can support myself, that there is a chance I can be happy again. Please, God, please just let me have hope for a little while.*

On my second day at work, I stopped by 7-Eleven to get a hot coffee. It was negative forty degrees outside, and I had to leave my car running. There are usually places to plug in your core heater in Anchorage so that your engine doesn't freeze. They didn't have that at 7-Eleven, and I only had one key for my car. Therefore, I left my car running when I went inside. When I got back outside, my car was gone. "Dammit!" I screamed. Could I ever catch a break?

I called the police and then I called the temporary agency to tell them I might be late for the insurance company job. I got a cab and made it to work on time, and the police found my car later that day. Someone had taken it to get wherever they were going and then ditched it. It really wasn't worth stealing. Because I made it to work, even though my car had been stolen, the temporary agency gave me an "Employee of the Month" award. I thought that this was a good sign that things were only getting better. Maybe hope was going to pay off...until it didn't.

The filing job was hard because I still struggled with reading and remembering stuff like numbers. I found that I was making a lot of mistakes. I knew I was going to get fired, so by one o'clock on my fifth day of work, I left so that I wouldn't have to face the indignity of being fired again. That last tiny bit of hope that I had the audacity to have was snuffed out like the artic sun. I knew I shouldn't have had hope. When you have hope, you can have it torn away and you will have even deeper despair and loss than you had before. I wanted to die. Some people might *say* they want to die, but I *really* wanted to be dead. If I could have wished it to be so, I would have died right there.

As I left the insurance company, I walked up the stairs and passed the glass wall where all the people with jobs were sitting at their desks, talking on phones and drinking coffee. I really, really, *really* wanted to be on the other side of the glass wall. I sat down on a bench and pretended to pick up a cup of coffee and take a drink. I even pretended like I was listening to someone tell me about the date they had the night before. That's all I wanted. I wasn't asking for much from life at all. *Why is life so unfair?* I thought. It wasn't *my* fault I had been hit by a car. It wasn't *my* fault I had amnesia. It wasn't *my* fault that I was so stupid. I was trying my hardest to keep this fucking job, and I just couldn't do it. I tried, and dammit, I couldn't do it again.

I got in my car and drove down the Seward Highway to Anchorage's south side, where the train tracks lead to Seward and Whittier. I was going to end this fucking suffering. I couldn't go on like this. There was nothing to look forward to, nothing. I was a stupid fucking retard who couldn't even keep a fucking stupid file clerk job. I was a fucking worthless piece of dog shit. I was insulting dog shit by saying dog shit was like me. I could get on the train tracks and wait for the train to Seward to run me over. It would be quick, and it would be over.

I parked my car on the side of the highway where the road meets the Cook Inlet. I had loved this place at one time, and it was as good a place as any to die. I could see that the train tracks had been cleared of snow. I walked to the edge of the road and stepped onto the snow and—*whump!* I sank up to my waist in soft, crunchy snow. On top of that, I was stuck. *Dammit! Just let me get to the fucking train tracks,* I thought to myself. It was only twenty degrees outside, so freezing to death wasn't going to happen very quickly. The Whittier train sped by, and so did my nerve for getting run over by a train. I lay back in the waist-deep snow and cried. I have no idea how long I cried, but I was getting cold and lost my nerve to kill myself. I wiggled my way out of the ditch onto the side of the highway and got back in my car. I was so fucking retarded I couldn't even kill myself right.

CHAPTER 9
The Man of My Dreams

I was way beyond lonely. I had always had a boyfriend since I was eighteen years old. I had never been a single person for more than a couple of weeks until now. *So* codependent, I know. This was a different kind of lonely. I was absolutely, 100 percent sure that no one would want to be my boyfriend again—no one to care about me, no one to spend time with, no one to love. What I was really looking for was someone to make me feel better. I was broken and sad, that damaged doll sitting in the bargain bin at a dollar store waiting for someone desperate enough to take me home. Be careful what you wish for because that is what I got.

I went to the Puffin Bar one night in Anchorage, desperate for any type of companionship. I ordered a Bud Light and a Bloody Mary. In Alaska, I had begun to drink a lot. I didn't want to feel anything. I had been so sad for the last few years. *Years!* Not days, not months. How can someone be expected to keep hope alive for years and years? My hope died when Stuart kicked me out of my own home to have me live with my parents.

Then it happened. When you are at your lowest, that thing you think you've been waiting for shows up. That thing that you think will make everything better. That man who will make the world okay again.

Three men about my age came into the Puffin, ordered a pitcher of beer, and began to play darts. One man had straight blond hair with a huge cowlick in the front, like me. When I saw Martin for the first time, my heart started beating so hard I got dizzy. He had blue eyes and a little blond mustache. His left pupil was much larger than the right one because, as I found out, he was in a motorcycle accident a few years earlier and was left with some brain damage. *Like me!* He was funny and spoke with a slight drawl.

"Hey, come over here!" he said to me. *Me? He was talking to me?* I thought. He offered me a glass of beer and asked me to play darts with him and his friends. *No way!* Martin was so handsome and funny. This couldn't be real. He lit a Newport cigarette and took a draw from it while putting his other arm around my shoulders. We talked for a long time and played a few rounds of darts. I was in heaven.

"Follow me to the bathroom," he said. I would have done anything to feel some semblance of normal, some moment of happiness.

When we got into the bathroom, he took out his keys and a tiny plastic bag. He dipped a key into the tiny bag and pulled up some white powder. "Hold one nostril shut and sniff this, like this," he said as he sniffed the white powder into his right nostril.

He dipped the key back into the baggie and brought it up to my nostril. Without any hesitation, I sniffed it in. I would have probably drunk gasoline at that moment if he had asked me to. Martin dipped the key back in the baggie and brought it up to my other nostril. I took a quick short sniff, and the key was clean. The powder burned slightly in my nostrils, and for the first time in years, I felt happy. The joy was instantaneous. Not a little bit happy—I was ecstatic.

Martin held the back of my head and pushed his lips against my mouth as we stood in front of the urinal in the bathroom of the Puffin. He moaned as he pushed his tongue inside my mouth. I was in heaven. What was this magical powder, and why had I not heard of this before? The sadness and loss were all a distant memory at that moment. I had a handsome man right there, and he wanted to be with *me!* We were having fun. *Why couldn't I feel like this all the time?* I thought. I asked Martin if I could get more of whatever he had. He told me he could get more, but he didn't have the $50 that it cost. I had $50 in my pocket. It was a no-brainer. I had cashed my last paycheck from the temporary agency, and I *really* needed this.

Martin took me to his apartment when the bar closed, and we stayed up until six in the morning. I was having the time of my life. Why had I not heard of this before? Martin said he uses it to be happy because of the brain damage he got from the accident. He told me about his life and showed me his Nazi memorabilia. At the time, I didn't know what a Nazi was. Looking back, I still don't quite understand how he was a gay Nazi. All I knew then was that Martin was in some club, and he showed me his outfit and some of the books and pamphlets for his club.

His boyfriend had kicked him out, too, after his traumatic brain injury. We had so much in common. I was happy for the first time in over five years. Not just a little happy but *amazingly* happy. I had fallen in love on that first night with Martin…and cocaine.

CHAPTER 10
The Awful Reality

Martin and I woke up in the late afternoon, and I was more sad and desperate than I had ever been. My body ached. My sinuses were swollen and burning. My eyes were puffy, and I couldn't think. *Why couldn't I always feel as good as I did last night Why?* I thought. I wasn't sad, I wasn't lonely. I was having fun for the first time in forever. I didn't have to think about having brain damage. I didn't have to think about being locked in a room by myself for two years. I didn't have to think about getting kicked out of my own home to be sent to live with my parents or my dad having cancer. I didn't have to think about shit. I got to just feel good, dance, talk with people, play darts, and drink beer. I have to feel that again. Knowing that a happy feeling is right there within your grasp when all you have felt is misery and sadness and desperation is impossible to pass up. Why would I not do whatever I could to not feel like dying every single day?

That evening, Martin and I got in my car and went back to the bar to get some cocaine. He then asked me to drive him somewhere and wait in the car. We drove to the parking lot of an adult bookstore. It was dark all the time in Anchorage that time of year. I sat in the car waiting for about three hours while Martin hung out in the back room, waiting to sell some part of his soul for money. I would have done anything so that Martin would stay with me. He was the only person in years who had shown any interest in me. Both of us were damaged goods, slowly selling off pieces of our souls just to not hurt all the time.

*****

Within a few weeks, Martin decided to get back together with an ex-boyfriend, Tom. Tom was big and buff, so I was alone again.

Most days, I would start by bringing one of the antiques Stuart had sent with me to a pawn store. I would go and wait at the Puffin for Steve, the bartender who sold coke. Sometimes I would sit there for up to seven hours drinking beer and waiting for Steve to get a stash delivered. I couldn't imagine going through an entire day without feeling good.

Over the next few months, I sold or pawned all of the furniture and antiques that Stuart had sent with me. I had begun using cocaine almost every day to keep from having to feel the withdrawal and misery.

I was at the Puffin one evening when a young Eskimo boy, about eighteen, sat next to me and put his hands on my knees and looked me straight in the face. "Do you know where we can get high?" he asked. No one had paid me any attention since Martin, and I longed to have some connection with any person. He was very handsome—straight, shiny black hair with almond-shaped eyes. His name was Eric, and his eyes were lit up with energy and playfulness. I really wanted whatever he was willing to give me.

"I have some coke," I said. He and I went to the bathroom and finished off the little baggie. He put his hands up the back of my shirt, leaned forward, and began sucking on my neck. I knew this wasn't real this time, but I needed it.

"Let's get a hotel room," he whispered in my ear. I had sold the antique French Rosewood bedroom set that Stuart let me have, and I still had a hundred dollars left from it.

My utter desperation for any companionship said, "Yes." We got in my car, and Eric said he wanted to stop at somebody's place who owed him money.

"I made a bet with this guy, and he owes me a hundred bucks," he told me. We pulled up to the back of an apartment building in Spenard and went to some guy's apartment where there were a couple people on couches, just lying there like they were dead. Eric told me to give him some money. He made some exchange with the one guy who was awake and told me to sit down. I had no dignity or decency left in me.

I sat and waited as instructed while Eric went into the bathroom for about ninety minutes. He came out, energized, and took me by the hand back to the car. "Let's get that motel room," he said devilishly.

We went to a motel on First Avenue, and I rented a room. Eric climbed straight into the bed, turned on the TV, and took out a small kit of some kind. "Come here," he said menacingly.

Eric had a spoon, a lighter, and a syringe with some blood on it. He took a tablet, smashed it, mixed it with some water, and lit the lighter under the spoon. He took the syringe and sucked up the hot golden-colored liquid. "Come here," he orderd.

I was not that person. I was not a junkie. I judged every other person whom I saw shoot up, and here I was. But I didn't care anymore. I let Eric poke the needle in the vein on my arm, and just like that, I was happy again, like the first time I did coke. I wasn't a retard. I wasn't destitute. I wasn't a stupid shit of a person who couldn't keep a job. I wasn't brain-damaged. I didn't have amnesia. For a few hours, I just was, and that's all I could hope for. Nothing was ever going to be good again in my life.

CHAPTER 11
The Beginning of the End

I got a temporary job assignment, answering phones and typing. I was a total wreck by then. By eleven o'clock, I would leave for lunch, go to the Raven, down four or five beers, shoot up, and go back to work. I have no idea how I did not get arrested. I was so high and drunk I would just sit there zoned out.

I went back to my parents' house to stay the night, and I wanted to get high so badly that I took a bunch of pills that my dad had for his cancer treatment. I have no idea what they were. They could have been anything. I just didn't want to feel anything. The sadness was so constant and so deep that I knew death was the only way out. I didn't wake up until noon, and my dad had called me in "sick" for my job.

My brother, Wayne, was still in high school. He yelled for me to come up from my bedroom in the basement. My aunt was there, along with my cousin, my dad, and my mom, and her best friend Margie. Everyone was looking at me. My sixteen-year-old brother, Wayne, had videotaped me the night before and was now having an intervention with my family. My little brother, who was struggling with our father dying of cancer, had the strength to also do a drug intervention for me.

"Sit down," my brother said in a firm voice. He turned on a video as we all stared at the TV. It was me but not me. I was dancing and flailing around the living room. I was high out of my mind, and my brother had recorded me. I was so ashamed and appalled by what I saw. So, so ashamed.

My very codependent mother looked at me in the face, tears running down her cheeks. Her eyes were so red and swollen from crying that I could hardly see she had eyes at all.

"If you don't get better, you can never come back!" she screamed at me over and over, looking me straight in the eyes. I knew she was serious. She had told me many stories of her own brothers' drug and alcohol problems and how her father would bail them out. She knew from decades of experience with her brothers that she could not endure what her father did with her own brothers.

I had tried mental hospitals and drug treatment facilities and was still a mentally ill, drug-addicted, brain-damaged homo. I look back and cannot believe how much my little brother, Wayne, had to love and hate me at that moment. I had wanted to die every day for the last three years. I had nothing left; my mind was gone. I had no semblance of dignity for a very long time. I had no hope for the future. I had no hope for ever being happy again.

CHAPTER 12
The First Miracle

I don't remember the time of year I arrived at the Pride Unit of St. Sebastian Hospital. I vaguely remembered how I got there. I had taken so many different drugs and prescription medications and had been drinking so much beer and vodka that the little bit of brain I had was drowned. That was, indeed, the idea after all. The drug treatment program that my brother had found was for LGBT people like me, on Medicare or Medicaid, with both an addiction and mental illness. You needed to have a dual diagnosis to be admitted. I had brain damage, amnesia, depression, drug addiction, alcohol addiction, and who knows what else. Truthfully, I only went because my family made me.

I arrived at the modest brick building in a cab from Chicago O'Hare airport. I don't know how I got to Chicago or even how I got in a cab, but I rode the elevator up to the third floor with the orderly. I was supposed to stay here for the twenty-eight days. Everything was very gray, cold, and industrial. There was a caged-in area on the roof with razor wire on the top of the fence. The orderly ushered me to the elevator, but all I saw was the angel of death escorting me to hell.

The elevator made a groaning sound as it went up the floors. I wanted to throw up or shoot up or get fucked up, but I didn't want to be here. It felt like I was going to prison.

Now *this* was a moment when I just needed something from the world—a sign from God, Allah, your higher power, Mother Earth, Buddha, Ganesh, whomever. Throw me a line, someone…anyone. *Please*. Give me a sign. *Something*. Because I *cannot* go on one more day on this earth if nothing is going to change. I *cannot* endure this pain, this indignity, this injustice. I can't. I am not strong enough. I can't have any more loss, any more sadness. I just can't, so please, just please send me a sign. I just need some tiny reason to even *try* to make things better. I *can't* do this by myself. I can't continue to be by myself. I am so lonely. I am so sad. Life just isn't fucking fair, and I need this one tiny sign that there is any hope for me to ever be happy again. I don't need a lot. Just please give me a sign, anything at all. I don't need much from life anymore, but please, to just not hurt all the time. I just…need…a sign…that *anything* is going to get better. My eyes burned from the tears that wouldn't come out. There have been too many tears. I have nothing left—no hope, no energy, not even fricking tears. I dry-heaved as the elevator jerked its way up to the third floor.

Time stood still. The elevator dinged at the third floor. The heavy gray doors slowly opened, but I couldn't see because my eyes were burning from the tears that wouldn't come out. It was dark in the elevator, but the ward I was heading to was brightly lit. And there it was, the first miracle. The doors clanged open, and there stood a skinny, younger-looking Black man with his arms stretched in the air. His body curved like a diva on stage, ready to perform.

"We have anotha sista!" he said dramatically. The universe pushed me forward into his arms, and I hugged the skinny man and sobbed like I had just come from the womb. Real tears began to flow. A friend. A real person who is excited to meet me for the first time in so long. And not because I had drugs or a little money or was some-one to have sex with. Just because I was a *person* who needed help.

CHAPTER 13
Group Therapy

Jerald had on baggy denim overalls and a yellow T-shirt that clung to his bony shoulders. He had smooth brown skin and big smile where all his teeth showed. His elbows and wrists were the biggest part of his arms.

"Gurl, where you from?" Jerald asked as he ushered me into a community room with a dozen chairs and a television set.

"Alaska," I said.

"Gurl, ain't that cold there? How'd you do it?"

"Not good," I said as my face cringed up as more tears began to well.

For the next twenty-eight days, I was to have intensive group therapy with mostly gay Black men who had drug and alcohol addictions, with depression or bipolar disorders. Most of whom also had AIDS. There were some lesbians and transgender people in our groups, and there were a few other White gay men and White lesbians. This was 1999 in Chicago, and the AIDS epidemic had wiped out more than half of the gay men who were fifteen years younger to thirty years older than me. Every couple of days, someone would leave, and others would join our group that ranged in size from six to twenty-four people.

For the first few days, I lay in the bed in my room. I was tired. I was tired of being high and then desperately sad and then high again and then desperately sad again. This is no way to be. For now, all I wanted to do was sleep, but that was not really allowed. Mentally,

I knew I did not want to do drugs anymore. Physically, my body screamed, "More! More! More!"

I stayed sick for the first couple of days, scratching my skin and throwing up. Several guys had come in with crystal meth addictions, missing teeth, boils, and lesions on their skin. One guy had picked out his hair, including his eyebrows, in a weird pattern after tweaking for the last few days on crystal meth.

One guy came in with schizophrenia. He didn't talk much, but I could tell what he was feeling. His eyes communicated everything. He had been taken in first at the Salvation Station where they shaved his long hair to a buzz cut. The Salvation Station wasn't a great place to get help if you were a schizoid and even worse if you were a gay schizoid. The Salvation Station does wonderful work, just not for gay people.

They sent him to this place after he wouldn't renounce his gayness. He had been high, drunk, and turning tricks to feed his addiction and quiet the voices in his head. I can't imagine what the monsters on the streets did with a schizoid who had no idea what reality was. He was even more of a target for abuse than I was, and I felt his pain. He had just come into the Pride Unit and was sitting in a chair next to the nurses' station, waiting to get his room assignment. He was shaking and mumbling. I was compelled to sit in the chair next to his.

I slowly leaned over and quietly said, "Hello." He looked up at me, tapping both of his feet on the floor so quickly it shook his whole body. I slowly reached over and took both of his hands in mine and held them. His feet stopped tapping, and his body shook less. He looked into my face, and I could see that he knew I was a kindred soul who knew the same pain and misery that was his reality. This was the first person I felt could understand my soul's anguish every day, someone I didn't have to say all the right words to for them to understand my pain and lack of hope—my misery, the reasons for my depravity. Having one person who can understand you is a big deal. Feeling that no one understands what you have gone through is a most awful feeling. I looked at my schizoid-brother in the face, and we both stared at each other, knowing for the first time in forever that one other person understood us.

As I soon found out, I was not alone when it came to having a really shitty life. Each day, the small group of people in my ward would gather in the TV room, sit in a circle, and talk about the things that we were going through. We'd also talk about the things that had happened in our past to fuck us up. Each time you have something bad happen in your life and you need to deal with it, all the old bad stuff that happened resurfaces as if to say, "I'm here too. Don't forget about me." That bad stuff never really goes away; you just learn how to deal with it better. All the people in my ward had some really shitty stuff happen in their lives. I guess they wouldn't have been in the Pride Unit if their lives were all awesome.

Many of the men had sold drugs and prostituted themselves to get more. Many had parents who were drug addicts or mothers who were prostitutes themselves. Several young men were cast out by their families or physically abused for being gay.

"You can beat away the gay," was a line one man said his family repeated regularly. When your family kicks you out at thirteen, fifteen, or seventeen with nowhere to go, you become prey to the monsters on the street. Those monsters fuck with you and fuck with your head until you need drugs to just not think about killing yourself every day.

It had been six years since my car accident, and I was beginning to remember things from my past. I was beginning to recall basic facts about some people and specific events. It was hard to know how much of my "memory" was learned from people telling me versus really remembering things. Some stuff could have stayed forgotten, however. I wish I had a button to pick and choose the memories to keep as they resurfaced. But as my life was generally shitty, the bad memories came back before any good ones did. I would have preferred to just never remember pre-1995 instead of bringing back some of these nightmares that terrorize me to this day.

In group therapy, I talked a lot about my accident, staying isolated in my room for years, and about how sad I was all the time. Before getting amnesia at twenty-seven years old, I had remembered several other things that I really wished I didn't remember. I had begun to believe that my life was cursed. I was being punished by God, and I thought I maybe knew why. I was gay, of course, but I did not believe that God was punishing me for this. I didn't remember my parents or grandparents ever making me feel bad about being gay. This was unique among my fellow recovering crazy people in the Pride Unit. I knew it had to be something else. What had I done? What had I not done? Unfortunately, I think I knew.

Throughout my late teenage years and twenties, I had a lot of accidents. I broke my ankle, cut off my thumb, was carjacked, held at gunpoint in a gas station parking lot, and had several car accidents. There are way too many bad events for there not to be *some* reason. I didn't experience a normal amount of bad or unfortunate things while growing up; I went from bad event to bad event. I was pretty sure that I had been a good student. I had several jobs, worked hard, didn't do drugs, or even knew anyone who did drugs. Why would I have such bad karma? As I said in the opening of this story, there are one, two, maybe three things—good and bad—that happen in your life to change everything. In group therapy, I talked nonstop about my car accident and the "first" bad thing that happened when I was younger. This I blamed as the root of my cursed life.

While I am writing this story, I will say that both my car accident and the event that I will share are events that are never gone from my mind and are the two most awful things that have happened to me. I struggle to write about the first, as even today, I don't remember everything. I don't remember the details. This could be because of the long-term amnesia, or it could be my brain's way of trying to protect me.

I do remember that there were several times I dealt with depression before my car accident ever happened. Every time I had a depressive episode, *this* event always raised its ugly face. "Remember me," it would say. "I'm still here, waiting to fuck with your head."

So here is my ugly, reprehensible truth for which I felt I could never be forgiven…

When I was thirteen years old, I believe that I was very responsible for my age. I took care of the majority of the daily tasks on our farm associated with feeding and caring for our twenty or so head of cattle. We also had an assortment of other animals on our farm— horses, chickens, ducks, and turkeys—that I also tended. I was so conscious of my responsibilities that I would often have nightmares about forgetting to water pens of chickens and turkeys. Then when I finally remembered, they would be dead and dying. This never happened, of course, but I had recurring nightmares while growing up. I later learned that these nightmares were a bad omen of unfortunate events in my future.

Being a responsible teenager sets you up with opportunities to babysit. I would occasionally babysit for a family down the road with two boys, ages three and five. I am crying now as I write this because even more than forty years later, this event ruined large parts of my childhood and fucked up the way I think.

I enjoyed babysitting and playing with kids. The two little boys were both blond-haired and blue-eyed like myself, like most people in Northern Minnesota. I would make them snacks, play with them, and put them to bed at their assigned bedtimes. After the boys went to sleep, I would clean their parents' house, wash any dishes, dust, and vacuum. I was super responsible and didn't think it was fair for me to just sit around after putting the kids to bed.

Sometimes their parents would come home, and it was obvious they had been fighting. Sometimes their parents would come home, and it was obvious they were drunk off their asses. As a thirteen-year-old living in a rural community, I had no references for what normal and not normal behavior was. This was until one night something unthinkable happened. As a child, my world was small, and I loved that. We didn't watch much TV. Our small-town radio station played Polish and Scandinavian polka music and maybe country-western. I knew nothing of the world with how fucked up things can be.

One evening, I walked down the road to babysit on a Friday night so the little boys' parents could go out to dinner and whatnot. I started the evening by playing with the boys like I usually did. I made peanut butter apples and made macaroni and cheese from a box. I put hot dogs in the mac and cheese to make it even better. We were playing Hungry Hungry Hippos and some board game in the basement when the five-year-old little boy looked at me squarely in the face and said, "Daddy puts his penis in my mouth."

Okay, time stopped here for a minute. *What did he just say?* I thought to myself. The little boy was five and missing his front teeth.

"Daddy put his penis in my brudder's mouth too," the three-year-old nodded his head up and down. I didn't know how to react, so I didn't. Why didn't I say something? Why didn't I react? Why didn't I ask some questions? They were three and five years old. How would they make this stuff up? We kept playing with toys. The little boys stated these facts to me in a way that seemed like they were asking me if it was okay. This was not real. Why was I not doing something, saying something?

It was getting late when there was a noise at the front door. Dammit! I realized it was past the boys' bedtimes, and I had forgotten to put them to bed. We were still playing board games in the basement when their dad came through the door without their mom. He was drunk or high or both. I had seen this before and started to explain and apologize for not having the boys in bed.

Then from nowhere, their father struck me in the face with the back of his hand and knocked me to the floor. *What was happening?!* I thought to myself. *Why did he hit me?* My head was spinning, and I couldn't react. He had been drunk before, but he had never... *What the fuck?!* The little boys started screaming. Their dad was a sizeable man, about forty, and I was thirteen and about ninety pounds. He fell on me with all his weight, and I couldn't breathe. He was yelling, but I couldn't tell about what. The little boys were screaming and crying.

What happened next would pollute my being for the rest of my life. Some things happen, and you can let them go. Some things happen, and you can *never* let them go. They ruin some part of what was good about you. It steals an innocence that can never be regained. A monster has found another victim and has consumed all that is good from them. This can't be happening. Why? Why? You will never, ever be the same person.

Their dad pushed down my pants. I still couldn't move; I was crying, screaming, begging him to get off me. "Please get off me. I can't breathe." I strained to get out. I tried to hit him backward, but I dislocated my shoulder. There was so much screaming. He penetrated me, and I screamed louder. It hurt like fire. His fat body was crushing me, and I couldn't breathe. *Why was he doing this?* I don't know how long this lasted because I went somewhere else in my head, like a rabbit that has been caught by a wolf, knowing this is the end for him, so he does not struggle. The rabbit knows to just lie limp in the wolf's mouth; the pain will be over soon.

After a horrible amount of time, the fat man rolled off me. I hurt all over. *Why? What had I done?* I did not cry. I did not scream. I was in shock. The little boys were still screaming. I tried to talk to them, tried to calm them down. I pulled up my pants, but my hands were shaking so much I couldn't buckle my belt. My back hurt. My shoulder hurt. My face hurt from where the fat man had hit me with the back of his hand. *What do I do?*

I need to get these kids out of here! I screamed in my head. *Now I must get them out!* I tried to pick up the three-year-old, but my shoulder throbbed from popping out of joint as I tried to hit the fat man backward.

"Walk! Follow me!" I yelled at them, but it only made them cry harder. My abdomen burned as I tried to pick up the boys simultaneously—one in my left arm and one under my right. I couldn't do it. What do I do? I was shaking, shaking so hard my teeth were chattering. Snot was running out of my nose. They weren't listening to me. I did a hard suck to clear my nose and my mind. My mind was racing. The fat man was passed out on the floor, groaning and making disgusting noises. This has to be what hell is like. *What do I do? What do I do? What do I do?* My mind was racing. *What, what, what?*

There are decisions that you make in your life that haunt you until the day you die. This was mine. Knowing now what I do, I would have done something different, but I didn't know any better at the time. I crawled up the stairs from the basement and went home, leaving the little boys there screaming with their father passed out on the basement floor. I walked, limped really, down the side of the road. I could hear the boys crying for about five minutes as I walked. It seemed like forever. I tried not to hear them, but my fate would be that I would hear them screaming for the rest of my life. I didn't even think about turning around to go back.

This is my biggest regret in my life, and this would transcend time and space to haunt me forever. I tell myself that I was only thirteen and there was nothing I could do. I had been raped and beaten. Deep in my consciousness, I still feel there is still no excuse for leaving those little boys there with that monster. The walk down the road was dark. There was no moon, and there were no stars. There were mosquitos, and it was hot. *This is hell. This is my walk through hell,* I thought.

When I got home, it was dark. I looked up at the sky. There were still no stars. There was still no moon, and the millions of stars in the sky were all hiding. I needed to see some stars, some light, some goodness. I told my mother what had happened. She could see I was hurt and bleeding from where the fat man hit me.

"Don't tell anyone!" she said excitedly and repeatedly. "If your father finds out, he will kill that man and go to jail." My mother was a very pragmatic person; my father *would* have killed him. He wouldn't have hesitated. Among other small enterprises, my dad was a gun dealer. He had an assortment of weapons to choose from to hunt the monster down and kill him. My father was very protective, and this would have been too much for him to even *pretend* he had any restraint. She told me to take a bath and go to bed, so I did. I tried to block this from my consciousness. I got in the tub and ran the water. I ran straight hot water and scrubbed and cried. *Why? Why did this happen?*

So now, my secret and my guilt were locked in tight, ready to mess with my head for the rest of my life. For a very long time, I believed this was why bad things happened to me. I was being punished by God for leaving those little boys with a monster. This was the first monster I encountered in my life. There would be many more. Monsters hide in society and disguise themselves as normal people. Our fat neighbor was the postmaster of our small town. Monsters are out there. Unfortunately, there were more to come.

I went to school the next Monday, and no one ever suspected what had happened to me just a few days before. No one. My aunts and uncles and cousins never knew. My friends never knew. My teachers never knew. I couldn't tell anyone. I didn't want my dad to go to jail for killing the monster. I had been raped and defiled and left two little boys with a monster who was doing the same things to them. Who was really the monster?

Guilt is a force unto itself. It's a funny thing that sneaks up on you. In group therapy, there were a few people whose stories led me to believe they could really understand me and feel what happened to me. Most of the people were everyday crazy drug addicts. Either they didn't have a clear reason why they were messed up or they just couldn't articulate it. It was always important for me to feel like someone could understand what I had gone through.

CHAPTER 14
The Boys in the Band

While I was in the Pride Unit at St. Sebastian Hospital, I met many people with stories as sad and tragic as they come. I didn't remember much about my past life except for a few stand-out, shitty experiences. The people I met while in the Pride Unit were the first people I actually knew and remembered. I had been very lonely, but much of this was because I didn't remember anyone from my past. I didn't remember that I had friends from high school and college or that I had cousins and neighbors that I grew up with. These were people I loved but didn't remember. I had to have met many people over the last six years with amnesia, but I couldn't remember most of them. This led to a very lonely existence. I probably knew a lot of people, but if I couldn't remember them, that begs one to question, did I *really* know them? I had a whole life that I had lived, but that life was gone. I didn't remember it, so it didn't exist. I was now like an infant born into a new world, discovering people and things for the first time.

As the drugs and alcohol cleared out of my body, my working memory improved. I was beginning to retain memories and information better than I had in a long time. When I met people, I could now remember them. Since everyone I met was in the same psych ward as I was, I realized that these people were a bunch of crazy, drug-addicted nutjobs. Still, I could relate to them and I could remember them. I could remember who they were and things they had told me. I now had a history with people. Crazy people, but they were someone. I wasn't lonely like I had been for the last six years.

I had been in solitary confinement in my head for six long years. I had been so lonely for so long. I guess mostly because I could never remember people long enough to feel like I knew anyone. While I was by no means "cured," things were moving in the right direction.

I could relate to one guy in our rehab ward who was driven to drug and alcohol abuse that arose from not wanting to be sad all the time. Davie had been adopted by a deaf couple from birth. They didn't want to have a baby that could be deaf, and they believed they had little chance of being chosen to be adoptive parents. As it happened, someone *did* choose them to adopt their son, Davie. One set of grandparents lived with them when Davie was a baby so that he could learn how to talk. As you would expect, Davie's parents loved him more than anything, and he felt it every day. He was spoiled and doted on and was growing up to be decent and kind.

When Davie was in high school, he had an evening job. One night, when he came home from his shift, he found his parents had been murdered. Apparently, deaf people are easy targets for criminals. Later on in his twenties, Davie got an apartment with his boyfriend. He asked his boyfriend to go to the corner store for ice cream one night. Unfortunately, his boyfriend never came home. He had walked into the convenience store as it was being robbed and was shot and killed. So much tragedy makes a person question, "Why me?"

To add insult to injury, Davie later contracted AIDS. This was 1999, and while there were some antiretrovirals available, they were expensive and didn't work for everyone. He was always sure he was going to die. Every time he got a cold, he thought it was the end. I understood his suffering, and I know he understood mine.

Most everyone in the Pride Unit at this time had AIDS, addiction, and mental illness. Most everyone was also Black and from Chicago. I didn't know much about anything, but I could see how terrible AIDS was. I could see how AIDS could cause severe depression, which could then lead to addiction. All these men thought they were going to die at any time. Many had no family support, or worse, their families abused and abandoned them. Some were abandoned as young as thirteen. How does a thirteen-year-old gay boy survive on the streets of Chicago? They do what they need to do to have food and a place to sleep.

Men would come in our unit so skinny their eyes looked like they would fall from their sockets. I know these stories were awful, painful, and raw, but these were people, and I hadn't really known anyone that I remembered well until now. I soaked up every story and every word. These people were my world. I found their stories sad and their spirits motivating. I was the first "White friend" many of these men had, and these men were the first friends that I remembered I had. One man, an oil rigger from Texas, had names for the color of everyone in our group—Paper-sack tan, tar-black, coco-puff, milk chocolate, and I was high-yellow. It felt nice to be included.

How did people see me at this time? I had stringy, long, blond hair. I don't think I had a haircut in years at that point. It was never a priority. I was simple and kind of dense. I didn't have any worldly possessions except for some jeans, sweatshirts, and a pair of gym shoes with holes in them. My clothes were raggedy and ill-fitting. Now that I was interacting with more people, I realized I didn't know about the things most people do. I didn't know about entertainers or current events. I didn't know about music or food types. Many of the people were into house music, and I had no idea what that was. I didn't know anything about the world or how it worked. I was simple and believed whatever people told me. I didn't understand most humor or sarcasm, and I think people laughed at me more than I realized.

Not everyone had dramatic events that led to their being there in that psych ward. Most of the men were about my age. There was one I remember named Rob. I never completely understood Rob's story, but I enjoyed listening to him when he talked. He was usually very positive and kind. He was tall, over six feet, with very dark skin and a scar on his forehead. He had an accent I would learn was a south-side Chicago accent, one with many Southern tones. Rob's mother was poor, and even though he didn't say it, I got the sense that he had been in foster care. His mom was obese and an alcoholic. Rob had six half siblings from his mom, each with a different dad. Rob was about thirty but still wanted his mother's love and attention. I don't think he knew who his dad was.

He didn't graduate from high school and worked as a waiter and a cook. In between jobs, he survived by "slinging dick," which I later realized meant he got money for sex, usually older men, Black and White, who were closeted. I'm not sure what I thought this meant at first, but it took me a while to understand what "slinging dick" referred to.

Rob had burns on his lips from a crack-pipe, and he was one of the few men at Pride who didn't have HIV or AIDS. His trauma was more hidden, but I could see it was just as real. Not everyone can put the finger on the exact thing that haunts their soul and causes them to have nightmares. Having a generally shitty childhood with long-term neglect can damage a soul as much as a car accident. It makes you wonder if you are worth anything and if there is anyone you can ever trust.

I was in the hospital ward for the entire twenty-eight days consistently with only one person, Essie. There were a lot of people coming and going. I heard people refer to the hospital ward as the St. Sebastian Spa and Hotel. I guess many people would voluntarily check themselves in after partying way too hard. They would lose weight, get sick, and then check themselves in long enough to sober up, clean up, and get some food in their stomach. Since they voluntarily checked themselves in, they could voluntarily check themselves out. I knew I wasn't going anywhere, as I had nowhere to go.

Essie had come in the day after I arrived. His boyfriend came to visit a few days later. Essie was a complete drunk, while his boyfriend was a nice, normal-looking guy. They had only been dating for a few weeks before Essie had been so drunk for so long that his boyfriend brought him into the Pride Unit. The day his boyfriend came to visit was the day he broke up with Essie. Not a real surprise, I guess. This was Essie's fifth time in the Pride Unit in the last seven years. I had no room to judge. This was my third treatment center in three years. I can't count the number of times I was in the emergency room at various hospitals around Anchorage.

With all that being said, Essie ended up being my roommate. He was slow, like me. I saw a lot of similarities in how people reacted to both of us. We were both somewhat developmentally handicapped.

Essie started getting drunk at seven years old because his father was an abusive alcoholic who would beat him, his sister, and his mother almost daily. Essie learned very early to sneak a bottle of beer from his dad and drink it under his bed to kill the pain. He was drinking beer daily by nine years old and was now thirty-something. His developmental impairments likely came from heavy drinking at an early age.

Essie's father had died years earlier, but he continued to live with his mother until she died just a few weeks before I met him. Essie and his mother slept in the same bed, a habit they had developed when the father would get drunk and pass out every night in the living room. Essie had been trying to get sober for at least ten years with limited success. He kept trying, which is all that really matters. He would talk a lot in group therapy about how much he missed his mother and how abusive his father was.

Then there was Daryl. Daryl was someone I was immediately intrigued with. I don't exactly remember him coming in, he joined one of our group therapy sessions one day. He didn't even *pretend* to like anyone. He was obviously very smart and very well read. He was also very angry and indignant to have to be in group therapy. He was stick-man thin, very tall, and very handsome with coal-black skin. He wore glasses and walked and sat very dignified. He had a white streak in the front of his shortly cropped afro.

Daryl's mother was a heroin addict. Her boyfriend was a heroin addict, and so were his aunts and uncles. Everyone I met pronounced heroin as "heron" like the bird with the accent on the second syllable. When I would hear "heron," I would always picture Alaska. Daryl's grandmother lived in the same building as he did and would take care of him. He said she would constantly beat him for being too Black. Daryl was gay, and so was his brother. His brother had died of AIDS early in the pandemic. His mother died of a drug overdose, and his grandmother had died of cancer. He now had no one, which made me empathize with him. Having no one is an awful feeling. Daryl found out he had AIDS after joining the military and was tested. He received a postcard in the mail telling him his diagnosis. Daryl was HIV-positive for ten years already and had thought every day he was going to die. I couldn't blame him for using drugs to try to not hurt every day. I felt his pain.

I met many people while in the hospital whom I remember fondly. There was a trans man who was morbidly obese and took advantage of women. He was in a wheelchair and very bossy and demanding. I cornrowed his hair while we were in the hospital, which is interesting because I'm not sure how I knew how to braid hair.

There was a lesbian who was so depressed that she could make everyone around her depressed. She had been molested by her father at a age and was still living with the trauma. There were several men who were prostitutes with regular clientele that they spoke of like a list of boyfriends. Many were "dope boys" who sold drugs on the street corners of Chicago. There were crack addicts, meth heads, drunks, and several who were mentally ill and became addicts. I saw extremely bipolar and schizophrenic behavior on a regular basis. Most were a complete mess, but these were the first people I could remember. I was so glad to know anyone. This is where my historical memory starts, the Pride Unit of St. Sebastian Hospital.

CHAPTER 15
The Purge

After my twenty-eight days detoxing in the Pride Unit of Lakeshore Hospital, I was moved into the Pride Apartments of a halfway house on the north side of Chicago. Three apartments in the building of thirty apartments were for LGBT people recovering from addiction and mental illness. There were four people to an apartment, with two people in each of the two bedrooms. There was a community room in the basement where we were all expected to attend daily addiction recovery meetings. Most everyone outside of the Pride Apartments was court-mandated to be in the halfway house; they were mostly straight, Black, and from Chicago. There were a few White, Hispanic, and other gay people in the rest of the building.

The apartments were coed, and on the weekends, many of the women would have visitation with their children, whom I found had been placed in foster care while their mothers were recovering from addiction issues. In the evenings, when we would all meet in the community room, I would listen to the stories of all the people I lived with in this halfway house. Many were sad stories. I couldn't imagine how it felt to lose your children to foster care. This was one tragedy that was new to me, and I hung on every word that people said. There was a lot of resentment, anger, and denial. There was also a lot of gratitude, hope, and support.

I was handicapped and damaged. I looked and sounded weird, but the people at the halfway house took me in like a family member when I had no one and nowhere to go. Rob and Essie were my room-mates. Rob was the one who taught me how to cook. The two of us had food stamps because of our handicapped status, so we would get food on the weekends and cook large kettles of collard greens with neckbones and macaroni and cheese. Then we'd share it with people in the building who didn't have food. We would get a bucket of chitterlings for special occasions, clean them, and boil them with a potato to take away the smell. I never knew there were so many types of hot sauce. We would serve the chitterlings alongside a large tray of spaghetti.

I enjoyed being with people. I had been so lonely for so long, and I was grateful to have friends and people to talk to. I enjoyed cooking and giving something back to the people who helped me. I *knew* what hunger was. I had gone without food or enough food before, and it was a humiliating experience. Seeing others with food when your stomach hurts from being so empty. Being so weak from hunger and not able to do anything about it. If I could share the food I had with someone who had none, I knew they would be grateful to not be hungry for at least one day.

During the weekdays, I would go to an outpatient program at St. Sebastian Hospital during the day. In the evenings, I would attend addiction meetings in the community room of our halfway house. Since my head was beginning to clear, I began to think of two things I needed to deal with. I had been receiving mail at the halfway house, but I hadn't opened any of it. I knew what it was. They were bills—*lots* of them—from doctors, hospitals, therapists, and clinics. I even had student loan bills thrown in there. I had no money and could not pay anything. I barely had enough for food and bus fare. I kept them in a cardboard box in my bedroom. Every day, mail would come, and I would simply put it in the cardboard box to deal with later.

I also had to figure out why I took so much medication. My head was clearing from detoxing from all the drugs and alcohol I had been killing myself with. Still, I was taking a lot of pills every day; I had fifteen different prescriptions for depression, anxiety, aches, pains, stomach, seizures, sleep—just so much medication. For me, getting clean and getting better meant that I also had to stop taking all the medication. I could do something about this now, so I simply stopped taking everything. While this wasn't the smartest thing to do and my doctors told me not to, I felt it was the right thing for *me* to do. I vomited every day for the first three weeks. I had been taking massive amounts of prescription medication for six years, and I had no idea if and what I actually *needed* to take. I went through massive mood swings. I was nauseated all the time. I was sad and depressed, then kind of okay, and then I would swing back to being horribly depressed. All this and I was *still* not going to take any more pills. I threw up at night, at outpatient, and while watching TV. I was so sick and nauseated, but I knew I needed to purge all these chemicals from my body. It took about a month to feel right, but I had won my first battle in taking back my life. I was in control of what I was going to put in my body, and it felt great.

CHAPTER 16
One Step Forward,
Two Steps Back

I had graduated out of the daytime outpatient program and was now going to the Pride outpatient program for three evenings a week. I needed to see if I could get a job. I had worked part-time at temporary agencies in Anchorage, but every job ended in disaster. I was really afraid I wouldn't be able to keep a job. Why would someone hire me? I was slow, made a lot of mistakes, and looked homeless. I signed up to do temporary work at a temporary agency in the Loop in downtown Chicago. I worked for a few days here and there, answering phones and checking people into buildings.

Then I got a part-time, temporary assignment as an administrative assistant at a large insurance company. Gail was my manager and a vice president of something. I had gotten a suit, tie, and dress shirt from the Brown Elephant, a secondhand store in Boy's Town, with clothing coupons from a local charity. I'm sure I looked disheveled and out of place when I showed up my first day. Gail was kind and made small talk with me. I told her that I had a master's degree in mathematics but that I was in a car accident and trying to get back on my feet. I probably disclosed too much personal information, but I don't exactly remember everything I told Gail. I worked there for my five-day temporary assignment when Gail asked me if I wanted to try another temporary assignment in the actuary team. I knew she was doing it out of kindness and that I was not qualified in any way.

Still, I smiled and said, "Yes, I would love to." That act of kindness touched me and motivated me more than Gail would ever know.

Gail assigned me to support an actuary manager, who happened to be albino. He was fifty years old with short white hair and bright pink skin. He was middle-aged and chubby with thick glasses. His computer monitor was the size of a big-screen TV, and he would go up close to it to read. I don't think he wanted to have to deal with me. I was still quite slow and dense, and I could tell he didn't like me. I would hear him say mean things about me to other people. I affectionately referred to him as the evil albino when telling my roommates about him.

My time with him didn't last very long. I was walking to work on my third week for the evil albino when two White teenage boys passed by me on the sidewalk and called me a retard. They had a football, and one of them threw it at me and hit me in the head. I was dazed, and they laughed at me. I had gotten a concussion from getting hit in the head and didn't make it to work. I was confused and angry. Why would someone be so mean? I didn't call the temporary agency because I couldn't remember anything. When the temporary agency got ahold of me, I had missed three days of work. I told them I had gotten a concussion but was fired for not calling in. Would those kids have hit me if they knew anything about me? If they knew how hard I was trying to keep a job? Maybe they didn't care. Maybe they were monsters-in-training. What they did was cruel, but I had to forgive them and focus on myself.

I missed a few days of outpatient therapy for my concussion, and when I returned, there was a new woman in our group. Tanya was lesbian and from Minnesota, where I had grown up on a farm. Tanya asked me to go out with her after therapy. I told her I was recovering from a concussion, but she insisted. After our group, I went with her in her truck, and we went to a gay bar. She ordered two bottles of 7-Up from the bartender, and then we stood at a table watching all the people as they came in. She had just driven from Minnesota to Chicago to get drug and alcohol outpatient treatment at Pride. She was staying with her aunt, who lived outside of Chicago.

Tanya was nice, but I was wondering why we were at a bar; we were two recovering addicts after all.

I soon found out why we were at a bar. Tanya nodded and side-eyed another lesbian from across the bar. They shook hands and greeted each other the way I used to greet my drug dealer at the Puffin Bar in Anchorage. Tanya had just bought coke. Misery loves company, and I guess that's why Tanya asked me to go out with her.

I should have walked away. I had a bus pass and I could have figured out how to get back to my halfway house. Instead, when she asked, "Do you want a bump?" I said yeah. I had six months being clean and sober. I had detoxed from all my prescription medication. I had gone to AA meetings, NA meetings, therapy, and addiction counseling every single day for six months. When the thought was planted to take a hit, I couldn't let it go. Coke made me feel so good, and right now, I felt shitty. I lost a good opportunity at the insurance company. I lost my job at the temporary agency. People are mean, and life isn't fair. What is one little bump of coke going to hurt?

I dipped my house key into the baggie and held it up to my nose. I sniffed hard but did not get that rush of pleasure I had wanted. Instead, I had a rush of fear. I was afraid and embarrassed. I didn't want to get kicked out of my apartment for using drugs. I had nowhere to go, and I can't sleep on the street. I turned around and left. Tanya never came back to outpatient at Pride. I guess she wasn't ready. I got back to my apartment and went straight to bed. I lay under my covers, awake all night from the coke, remembering all night how awful it was to be high and not able to sleep and then to be coming down from a high and *still* not be able to sleep. I was craving more coke, but there was no more. My nostril burned, and I sat up all night bargaining with God to please let me get through this.

CHAPTER 17
Lorna Doone

I started going to Alcoholics Anonymous meetings and Narcotics Anonymous meetings down Harlem Avenue. I had a bus pass, and the bus would take me straight down Harlem to the clubhouse. Harlem Avenue divides Chicago from its western suburbs. The club was on the Chicago side of the street. It was mainly a Polish crowd, and being half Polish, I felt somehow at home. I had gone to the meeting a few weeks in a row when I was stopped by an older woman. Lorna was about sixty years old with a bobbed haircut, several layers of rather unkempt dresses and shirts, 1950s-style glasses, and very yellow teeth from decades of heavy smoking.

"My name is Lorna Doone, like the cookie," she introduced herself very loudly. "Lorna Doone. I'm an alcoholic, and no one will be my sponsor, ya, no one," she said very dramatically.

"Hello," I said.

She continued, "I have three days of sobriety. Three days. Only three days. My last sponsor dropped me, ya, she dropped me. Oh-ho-ho," she wailed in a somewhat fake-sounding cry.

"I have one year of sobriety today," I told her.

"You do!" she yelled in very exaggerated fashion. "I'm so proud of you. Will you be my sponsor?" She lit a generic brand cigarette with another cigarette still burning in the ashtray in front of her.

At this time, a man had come into the club, apparently looking for Lorna.

"My Teddy-weddy teddy bear!" Lorna yelled at the man. Teddy was the same age as Lorna, about 350 pounds, and his belly stuck out from under his sweatshirt that was covered in a lot of food stains.

"Come on, Lorna!" he yelled at her just as exaggeratedly as did and then smiled, scrunched up his face, bent over, and stuck his tongue out at her. Teddy had a mop of gray, greasy, wavy hair with a five-day gray beard.

"This is my husband," said Lorna. "We're married. My mother didn't want me to get married, but I got married to my Teddy-weddy teddy bear." At first glance, Lorna and Teddy may have appeared to be drunk, but in fact, they were both developmentally disabled.

I became an AA sponsor for the first time this day with Lorna Doone as my sponsee. Lorna needed a sponsor, and I needed to be needed. I talked to Lorna on the phone every day and started going to a meeting a week with her. She was loud, obnoxious, struggled with staying sober, and became my friend.

Lorna was handicapped but didn't let that stop her from living her best life. The first time I went to visit Lorna at her apartment, I was horrified and amazed. There was garbage everywhere. Teddy showed me his bedroom, and he had filled it with cardboard boxes with a path that led to a cardboard cave. He hid his stash of comic books deep in the crevasses of the cave. The apartment smelled of stale cigarettes and body odor.

Lorna told me that her mother had been the first female executive at a large catalog retailer and had left her a lot of money. Lorna didn't know who her father was and believed her mother had been raped while on a business trip in Germany. Lorna's mother would always tell her that she could do anything she wanted. Lorna had graduated from high school, spoke fluent French and German, and had attended art school in Chicago. She painted with oil, and I thought her work was really good. Not just really good, amazing actually. She had paintings on all the walls in her apartment.

Lorna was needy, loud, and messy. She had terrible personal hygiene and was always overly dramatic. At this time in my life, she was a role model to me. She was dealt a poor hand, but she was doing everything she wanted to unapologetically. She graduated from high school and then attended art school. Her artwork mesmerized me. Painting was her passion, and Teddy was her muse. There was a giant nude watercolor, squarely in the middle of her largest wall, of Teddy lying on his side with all his hairy parts showing for all to see. She had captured his childlike innocence in his facial expression perfectly. I was nothing but impressed. She found a man who obviously loved her and got married. She found someone who loved her and whom she loved. That is a big part of life and of being happy. If Lorna could do all this, why couldn't I? Messages from God come all the time; you just have to hear them. God spoke to me through Lorna, saying, "You can be happy too. It's all up to you."

CHAPTER 18
Miracle #2

I lived in the Pride Program apartments for a year on the north side of Chicago. When it was time to leave, I had nowhere to go. I don't remember how it happened, but I moved in with Daryl, who was also in the Pride program.

I met Daryl in the Pride program at St. Sebastian Hospital. Daryl had contracted AIDS in the 1980s when he was in high school. So did his brother. Daryl always compared me to his brother and believed that we shared something. Daryl's brother died shortly after contracting AIDS, and much to Daryl's chagrin, he lived. Daryl was diagnosed with drug addiction, depression, and borderline personality disorder. This was my first introduction to borderline personality disorder.

While Daryl had AIDS and drug and alcohol addiction, the borderline personality disorder was what relegated him to a life of living on disability. Daryl would get a job, get angry at something, and then quit or get fired. He could not take any type of criticism or feedback without being compelled to get retribution and retaliation. Daryl was damaged goods, too, but he offered me a home when I had nowhere to go. He was desperately lonely, as he really couldn't tolerate people, and I was desperate to not be homeless. I was still simple, and at this time, none of his bad behaviors even registered to me.

Daryl had a Section 8 apartment on the far west side of Chicago. Section 8 was a housing program in Chicago that provided low-income people with a place to live. We had no furniture or really any worldly possessions. We found a couch and a mattress in the alley that someone was throwing away, and we carried it up to our apartment. We would go to the Brown Elephant, a secondhand store in Boy's Town, to find things we needed. A secondhand store is everything to someone who has very little. I found dishes, a few pots, and some pans. I could afford some clothes, so I had more than the two pairs of pants I had worn for the last two years. I also found a used Mac computer for $5, and I brought it home. That was the same price as two Big Macs, so it was quite a good deal.

I know we had nothing but each other's friendship and support. I was still struggling to learn to do things. I kept practicing reading and writing. I also practiced doing math. I had a spiral notebook and some pencils. I would practice math calculations almost every day. I had to relearn addition tables, multiplication, and how to do basic calculations. I would spend hours and hours writing math problems. I had been fired from a series of jobs in just the last six months, but I was happy. I had food, I had a safe place to sleep, and I had companionship. This may sound too basic to most people, but to me, it was everything.

We lived on the farthest western edge of Chicago and would take the bus from the Loop. I was taking the bus home one afternoon from a job that wasn't going particularly well. It was that time of day when the sun is low in the sky—right where it makes everything look a warm goldish, rusty-red color. It was spring, and I was carrying my coat. There were a lot of puffy clouds in the sky; the low sun cast a turquoise and melon-colored pattern across the clouds. I was focusing on the beauty of the clouds as I walked from the bus stop to our apartment.

There are times when God, Allah, Buddha, Mother Earth speaks and you must listen. I honestly don't know if I had missed messages before. I would like to think not, but as my life had been shitty for a very long period, I would have to consider the possibility that I might have. As I noticed the beauty of the clouds, a peaceful feeling settled over me. A ray of light appeared from behind a cloud that blinded me for a second, and then I got a calming feeling like everything was going to be all right.

Then… I heard a voice. "I know who you are," said the voice. The voice was low and quiet, like a whisper. I looked to the sky at the turquoise and melon-colored clouds. There was no one around me, but I heard the voice clearly; the voice was low and almost felt like a vibration.

"I know who you are," I heard again. I could feel the voice inside my head. I stopped and looked across the sky, thinking that I could see the being who was speaking to me. I felt calm, and tears began to well in my eyes.

"I know who you are because you are me," I heard for the third time. A warm feeling enveloped my body. I spun and looked around to make sure I wasn't crazy. I knew from that moment that everything was going to be okay. I don't know why and I don't know how. It was a message from God, and I wept tears of joy. Tears of joy! Not sadness, not loss, not pain. Call it what you want. Believe or don't believe. This is not for me to convince you. I knew everything from that moment forward was going to be okay. I don't know how I knew, but I believed everything was going to be okay.

I ran the rest of the way home, sat down with my new-to-me Mac computer, and found a job opening for a statistician at Apogee Food Company. I don't exactly know what compelled me to apply for this specific job. I didn't ask questions; I just started looking for jobs without overthinking anything. I don't know why I had the courage to even think I could get or keep this job. I had been practicing math problems, but they were simple math problems. I had had thirteen different part-time and temporary jobs in just the last nine months. I applied for this job and only this job. I had not applied for a real, full-time job since before my car accident. I took a leap of faith.

I started this job three months later as a full-time statistician in Research and Development for Apogee Food Company working on cheese and dairy products. I had gotten a real job for the first time in seven years! Now I just needed to keep it. This was miracle number two.

CHAPTER 19
A-P-O-G-E-E, Please Don't Fire Me

I had saved up money from my disability checks to buy a car for $500. It was a black two-door Chevy Nova. It was a complete junker, but it ran. I bought it from a young man who had come to Chicago from Peoria, Illinois, to get away from his parents and be his best gay self. He had gotten several parking tickets with the car and didn't need one to get around. I needed a car to get to this job. Being able to find a car that worked for $500 was very lucky.

Of course, my luck was improving but still wasn't great. Daryl had T-boned my new car coming out from our apartment just a few days after I bought it. I was starting my first real job in just a week, and I was going to have to make it work. I had taught Daryl how to drive, which may have been a mistake. He had *extreme* road rage. If he got upset at another driver, he would throw things out of the car window at the other car—coffee mugs, CDs, books, whatever was within reach. My car still ran, but the driver's side windows were busted, and the driver's door wouldn't open. I duct-taped clear plastic to the inside of the windows so the rain wouldn't get in. On my first day of work at Apogee Food Company, I arrived early and drove into the parking lot to the farthest space from the building. I didn't want anyone to see my car and ask any questions. I wanted to be seen as normal. I hadn't been "normal" for so long that I was afraid everyone would be able to tell that I wasn't.

My manager was a kind man with graying hair and a rattail, perhaps a bit hippy-esque. Frank was my boss's name, and he asked me to shadow my new coworker for a while to get up to speed on the job. I quickly realized that I hadn't learned about statistics, statistical terminology, or even enough about computers. I had taught myself how to read and write again. I learned the basics of using a computer and I had relearned basic math, but I literally knew *nothing* about statistics. My résumé said master's degree in applied mathematics, which includes advanced math, statistics, and computer science. My brain was still saying, "Five times six equals thirty, good job!"

I couldn't lose this job. No one here knew I had brain damage. No one here knew I was a recovering drug addict and alcoholic. No one here knew that I lived in an empty Section 8 apartment with a couch and mattress pulled from the trash or that my car was a T-boned junker. No one knew that I was recovering from amnesia, that I had lived in a psychiatric halfway house for a year, or that I had lost thirteen jobs. I really wanted a chance at a real life again. *Please, brain, don't mess this up*, I thought to myself. I had been fired from at least six of my part-time jobs in the last year, and I thought I could keep every one of them when I started. None of these last jobs was as hard as this job was. What was I thinking when I applied for this job? I had been an administrative assistant and general office worker at several places, and I was let go. I was really going out on a limb to think I could do this job. *Please, please, please give me strength*, I prayed silently as I went into the bathroom and sat in a stall. I said the "Our Father" and the "Hail Mary" repeatedly, as these were the only prayers I could remember.

*****

Glenbrook was such a beautiful place. The streets were clean, and people had yards with trimmed hedges and fancy trees. This was a faraway land as compared to the drug dealers and prostitutes I would encounter on my way to and from the train on the west side of Chicago to my last jobs in the Loop. There was no graffiti, trash on streets, or junker cars—except mine.

The drive to Glenbrook from the west side of Chicago was like being transformed to Cinderella each day. I would get to go to the amazing building with groomed hedges, and there was a pond with swans in the front. I could pretend that I was just like these people. I knew in reality I was never actually going to be like any of them. I was really trying to be normal, but too many things had happened in my life. I was never going to be able to relate and feel like I fit in. These people were all very nice and very smart. After work, I would go back each day to our section 8 apartment with no furniture—junkies outside our back door. I would go to an AA or NA meeting every day after work with all the other people who were just trying to fit in.

No matter what, I was determined that I was not going to lose this job. I would go to work each day two or three hours before everyone else got there. I had found a book called *Statistics for Dummies* at Barnes & Noble bookstore. Wow, was this an appropriately titled book or what? I would read the book on weekends and evenings. While I technically had a statistics job, a software package really did all the work. With each project that I got, I was able to stay ahead of it with my *Statistics for Dummies* book. That book saved my life.

For the first two years, I was terrified that people were going to find out who I really was. At the time, we all had phones on our desks with a red light that would light up if someone had left you a message on voice mail. Every morning for the first two years, I was terrified if the light on my phone would be red when I would come into the office. I couldn't just pick up the phone and listen to see what the message was. I had to get up enough courage each morning to accept the fact that I may have really messed something up and that I was found out. Then I would get fired again. If I had gotten fired, I would have probably killed myself this time. It would have been too much of a letdown for me to bear. For the first two years, I was a fraud pretending to be a statistician. My *Dummies* book was really doing all the work.

I have said before that there are monsters pretending to be people, waiting to take advantage of a moment to get pleasure from terrorizing you, waiting to tear away a little bit of your soul to feed their evilness. There are also angels disguised as people. My boss, Frank, was my first of several angels that would help me on my journey. He was kind, and I think deep down he knew I could do this job, but I just needed lots of help to get started. Frank changed my life and my trajectory. I can never repay his kindness and help. I really needed him at this time. I had lost *so* many jobs in just the last six months, not to mention in the last three years. Each time, I was humiliated and dejected, but I had to try again.

I had three coworkers who worked for Frank. They were also my angels. They were kind and never made me feel like I didn't fit in. Looking back, I know I was "weird." I didn't understand a lot of statistics, and my personality had issues. I still had my myoclonic seizure disorder that would activate at the most inopportune of times. I was moody and had a short temper. My three coworkers supported me through my journey to keeping a job so that I could support myself.

Why did this job finally work out? Was I finally ready, or was it that I just needed to find the right person to help me? Probably some of both, but years later, I sent a note to Frank telling him what he did for me. He may not ever have known that he saved my life that day he asked me to interview for a statistic job at Apogee Food Company in Glenbrook, Illinois.

There are bad things that set a trajectory in your life, and there are good things that do the exact same thing. This is the event that set a clear *before* and *after* for the better. More amazing things would happen in my life, but this is the single event that changed my life for the better. Without it, nothing else good in my life would have ever been possible. I finally had a chance to support myself. I had some dignity again. It had been seven years since I was hit by a blue truck on Interstate 80 in Omaha, Nebraska. I still didn't remember much of my life before 1995, and what I did know wasn't that great. This was amazing. I took a photo of myself on my first day at Apogee Food Company, the day that set my life on a positive trajectory for the first time in more than seven years. Say, "Cheese!"

Chapter 20
Biri and Carol

I am a codependent and I don't really like to be alone. I can make all the excuses and have all the rationale in the world. I was locked in a room by myself for two years. I was so lonely for six years that I tried to commit suicide. Whatever the reason, I just don't like to be by myself. After Daryl left, I went one evening to a gay bar in Oak Park, Illinoi—the Nut Bush. This was a smaller neighborhood type of bar, similar to those in Chicago. I sat down and ordered a Diet Coke. A small-framed, very pleasant, younger-looking guy sat next to me.

He had a happy, somewhat goofy expression and said, "I DJ here sometimes. Do you like house music?" He made a slightly silly face and did an exaggerated dance move. "My name is Birikoran Raheem Blacksmith, but you can call me Barry." There was something in his voice that was unfamiliar, and I thought maybe he or his family was foreign. Biri was funny and very emotive. He liked to talk, dance, go to movies, and eat out. Biri was nice, and he was fun to be with. I couldn't have asked to meet someone better. Biri and I went out a few times before he asked me to meet his mother. Biri lived with his elderly mother, Carol.

I picked up Biri to go out one evening and stopped in to meet his mother. "I'm Carol, it was nice knowing you," she said. She, like her son, had an odd sense of humor. Carol was a large woman with a neckerchief tied on her head and a floral house dress or muumuu. She had diabetes and arthritis, so she didn't stand up.

Biri and I went to a movie and then dinner at Flanagan's Restaurant. The server came to our table, and I ordered. She asked Biri what he would like to order.

"I'd like a cheeseburger, yah, yah, a cheeseburger," he said as he scrunched up his goofy face and squinted his eyes. I couldn't help but notice the startled reaction of the server. I had noticed similar reactions from people as Biri and I would go places, but I didn't think anything of it. Maybe they were trying to figure out his accent too.

Things that are perfectly obvious in hindsight aren't necessarily obvious at the time. Right then, I realized my new boyfriend was mentally challenged, or more politically correct, learning disabled. I later found out from his mother that he had an IQ of 79.

Okay, so Biri was different. I had begun to love him. He was simple but he was safe. He wasn't going to hurt me and he was definitely not going to lie to me. He was a hard worker and an underdog. I could relate to that. Biri was good-looking but just a bit goofy. I loved his mother, Carol, too. She later became my best friend.

My job was going well at Apogee Food Company, which was a surprise and a relief. I was getting a real paycheck for the first time in forever. I had kept the cardboard box with all the bills I had collected for the last year and a half, and I was now ready to look at them. When I started opening bills, I had no idea what to expect. Absolutely no idea. I had had amnesia for so long that I had no idea who many of the doctors were. I had a notebook and started writing down each debt. I had Medicare from being disabled, but this only covered 80 percent of each bill. I still had the 20 percent to pay myself. There was no way to pay for any of the doctors, tests, and hospitals with no income.

I got to $20,000 before I had to stop and look in amazement that I only opened a small number of bills. The pile was huge as each debtor sent the same bill each month now for over eighteen months. I kept opening letters and writing down numbers—$40,000 in bills, $50,000, and then $70,000. What the heck! How could anyone be expected to pay all of this? My medical bills totaled $82,603.54. This was more than double the average household income at the time.

For the next four years, I lived frugally and paid as much as I could to all the doctors, clinics, labs, and hospitals. I could have filed for bankruptcy, but morally, I believed that all the people who took care of me deserved to be paid. I was recovering from being severely handicapped, addicted to drugs and alcohol, and having complete amnesia. All those medical providers played a part in my recovery. They all deserved to be paid. Not paying them would have conveyed a lack of gratitude to the universe, and I was more grateful than any of my creditors could ever know. I paid every cent I owed because I was grateful.

CHAPTER 21
Children's Home and Care Society

In 2006, I bought a condominium in Forest Park, Illinois, just outside of Chicago. It was a small town holding the world record for the town with more dead than alive. Our town had acres and acres of cemeteries. Kind of weird notoriety, but the small downtown was nice and walking distance from my condo.

I finally felt like I had regained much of what had been lost. I had a good job, my own place, and a partner, Biri, whom I trusted and enjoyed spending time with. Biri was often silly and goofy, which would always make me smile when I felt down. While I still didn't remember much about my life, precar accident, I was very grateful to have the new life I had created. I was grateful to have a job where I was not constantly afraid of getting fired. I was grateful to be able to work again at all and to be able to function in a work environment.

While I had a job and a new home, I do know that I still had some psychological problems and deficits. I would have bouts of depression that would leave me white-knuckling it for days at a time. I would literally have to sit in a chair and tell myself, "This isn't real. This depression isn't real. I am good enough. I have friends. I have a good life. I can keep a job." At those times, I really, really wanted to act out in some way when I would get depressed—get drunk, find drugs, hook up with strangers—just to fill the emptiness I was feeling at that time. Biri was my rock when I would struggle with sadness and just needed someone to sit with me. After a few hours or sometimes a few days, the depression would pass, and I could go on with my life. I never ended up sabotaging anything, but there were a few close calls. Still, I did go on with my new life. Over the years, these depressive episodes would come less frequently with less intensity, but they would always be there.

Though I was very grateful for the life I had regained, I still felt like something else was missing. I was sitting in my cube at work one afternoon when I realized what I needed. I still had a tear in my soul, and it was eating at me. I had one great regret in my life to this point, and it was that I had walked away from those two little boys whose father was molesting them after I had been raped and beaten by the same man at thirteen years old.

Although I had processed this horrible thing in therapy for years, I still held myself responsible for not doing anything to help those kids. It is an awful fact, and this horror was never far from my consciousness. It was too late to do anything for those two little boys, as they would now have been young men. Did their father continue to molest them? Did they remember what had happened the night their father came home drunk, the last time I ever saw them? Were they okay? I had no right to ask them now or to interfere with their lives. That would have been a selfish act that would have no positive impact on the boys who were now young men.

I still needed to do *something* to right the wrong I had done more than twenty years earlier. I needed to make it right with the universe and right with my soul. I decided that I wanted to adopt a child who had been neglected and abused and needed a home. I would be the parent they needed and would save a child since I was not able to save the two boys when I was thirteen. Once the thought came to me, I couldn't stop thinking about it. I needed to be a parent to a child who needed a parent. It had recently become legal for gay people to adopt children in Illinois. I could right the wrong from so long ago and have a family of my own. These moments of clarity are few, and you can miss them if you aren't paying attention. This hit me, and then I couldn't get it out of my mind. I knew exactly what I had to do. I needed to adopt.

I didn't realize how humbling it was to really, really want something and have that decision be out of your control. When I finally realized I wanted to be a parent, I *really* wanted to be a parent. There are at least three different options you can take when you want to adopt a child. One, you can apply at an adoption agency where birth mothers chose the parents for their child. As a single gay man, I didn't think this was going to be a very likely way for me to adopt, and babies were easy to place with good families. Two, you can go through an agency that does international adoptions, but many countries prohibit single people from adopting children from their country. Many people were going to Russia, China, and India to adopt young children who had been living in orphanages for some time. Three, you can go through the foster care system to adopt children who have been removed from their parents for abuse or neglect. This was exactly the way I needed to do it.

I decided to go through the Illinois foster care system to become a dad. Even though it had recently become legal for gay men to adopt in Illinois, there were a lot of roadblocks. For the first several months, I combed through agencies and set up interviews with social workers. I was laughed at, told I was disgusting, and was told more than enough times that I would never be a parent. I had found an adoption agency near my home and made an appointment for an interview. When I sat down in an office with an older social worker, we began to discuss why I wanted to be a parent.

When I told her I was gay, she stood up and literally yelled, "We don't accept people like you. You are going to have to leave." Then she shooed me out of her office. As I walked out by the receptionist, I told her what had happened, and she said, "Baby, at least she told you to your face instead of leading you on for years." That was the truest thing I ever heard. She was right. That bigoted woman could have led me to believe I was in the running to be a parent and just let me linger, hoping I would lose interest. Each social worker I met held the key to my getting to adopt a child.

Then I found the Children's Home and Care Society. There are literally dozens and dozens of agencies that subcontract to the foster care system in Illinois. I had called and talked to more than ninety people and agencies when I finally found Children's Home and Care Society. When I called, I told them I wanted to adopt a child.

They said, "You have come to the right place." When I told them that I would be adopting as a single gay man, I held my breath, waiting to hear some nasty comment or to hear the phone hang up. Instead, they said, "No problem. We've recently placed several children with single gay men." *Where have you been for the last eighteen months?!* I shouted in my head. Finally, some hope had come.

CHAPTER 22
Mother's Day

"Hello, this is Cheryl from the agency," said the voice on the line. I received a call at work, and Cheryl was the Children's Home and Care Society social worker that I had been working with to get the needed paperwork to apply to be a foster-to-adopt parent. "I have some good news for you," she continued. "We have some twin African-American boys here, and they will be free for adoption very soon. They're two and half years old, they both have developmental disabilities, but you can have them if you want. Their names are Vincent and Vance."

It had been eighteen months of rejections, insults, dead ends, and disappointments. All of that was erased when I heard that there was not just one baby but twins, and I could be their dad. All I wanted to do at that moment was see them, pick them up, and hold them.

I scheduled a time to see them in two days at the adoption agency. I did not care the least if they were little Einsteins or mentally challenged. Boys or girls, Black or White, big or small—I didn't care. I wanted to be a dad, and they needed a dad. I needed to be *their* dad. They were going to be my babies!

I found that 75 percent of the children that needed to be adopted in Illinois were African-American boys. White parents were the majority of parents adopting. They usually wanted a White girl, then a White boy, then a Black girl. Black boys are at the end of the list. In Illinois, it was unusual for Asian or Hispanic kids to be adopted from foster care by people who weren't relatives. I also found that there are adoption agencies for Canadians to adopt African-American children from the United States. I wanted to adopt kids who needed to be adopted the most. It was harder to place multiple kids together, especially Black boys and kids with disabilities. I was meant to be their dad, no question.

I could not sleep for the next two nights. I was so excited to meet *my* kids. I had a two-hour drive to the visitation center. I had bought the boys each a toy they could sit and ride on, along with a stuffed animal for comfort. I was so nervous.

When I met them, I didn't want to leave. Vincent and Vance were playing in a visitation room when I arrived. I didn't know what to think. They were so little and adorable. They had matching outfits with jean pants with elastic waistbands with their diapers sticking out the back. They each had on a red T-shirt with little red sneakers. I slowly walked into the room, not knowing how to act.

Then Cheryl, the social worker, rounded up the boys in front of me and said, "Boys, this man wants to be your dad." For the next hour, I knelt on the floor and pushed trucks and flew airplanes. I built towers of blocks and talked for stuffed animals. There was no turning back; I was going to be Vincent and Vance's dad. I knew it from the moment I saw them. I fell in love with these babies from the first time I saw them.

For the next six months, I got to have them every weekend from Friday at 5:00 p.m. to Sunday at 5:00 p.m. I would drive down to their foster home two hours south of Chicago and pick them up. I had to buy car seats and diapers before picking them up for the first time, but I didn't mind. I took them to McDonald's on the drive back and got them cheeseburgers. Each of them ate five sandwiches! I had no idea how much a couple of two-and-a-half-year-old kids should eat, but they seemed to eat a lot.

When I got back to our condo for the first time with the boys, Biri tried to interact with Vincent and Vance, but he was not that interested in kids. When I started this process, I asked Biri if he was okay with getting kids.

He said, "You do what you want." I guess that wasn't an actual supportive statement. After the first few weekends with Vincent and

Vance, Biri gave me an ultimatum. He told me that I had to choose him or the boys, but I couldn't have both. Biri and I had been living together for two years, and he was with me during the whole eighteen months of rejection. "I said it was okay because I didn't think anyone would ever let you have kids," he explained.

I loved Biri but I loved these babies more, even though I had just met them. I could not picture my life without them. Not for a second. Every time I even thought about what could go wrong with the adoption, I had an anxiety attack. While I was at work one day, Biri took all of his things and moved back to his mom's apartment. I later understood that Biri was afraid that when the boys grew up, they would realize he was handicapped and would be embarrassed by him. My heart hurt when I found that out. I worried, too, that the boys might be picked on for having a gay dad or for having a White dad. That was something to worry about later. For now, I would just be the best dad I could be.

For the next three years, my life revolved around raising Vincent and Vance. I was told that they were developmentally disabled before I saw them for the first time. They were definitely very small. Vance weighed twenty-one pounds, and Vincent weighed twenty pounds at almost three years old. Before I adopted them, Vincent and Vance would hide cookies in their diapers on the weekends with me. Their doctor told me this was a sign they had been left without food somewhat regularly.

I had to have them tested before the adoption would be finalized and found that they had severe malnutrition and that Vincent had chronic sinus infections. Vincent had been on antibiotics for the last year. He always had green snot coming from his nose and, at almost three, hadn't learned to speak because he couldn't hear. Vance would speak for him.

They were placed with me as their full-time parent on their third birthday. Vincent had surgery on his nose and ears shortly after that and started learning to speak quickly. Within a year, each boy had gained ten pounds, and they had many friends at day care. They were not developmentally disabled; they had been starved and malnourished by their former foster parents. That made me so angry.

When Vance was first placed with me, he would tell me about getting "whooped" by his foster parents. There would be no "whooping" here. Who would "whoop" a two-year-old? I had my babies. Vincent and Vance were on the mend, and so was my soul.

I was a dad. How was this even possible? I would sit in amazement, watching Vincent and Vance play, and think about where my life had been just seven years earlier. It had been seven years since my brother did an intervention and my family sent me to the Pride program for addiction and mental illness. After experiencing so much pain, there was now joy. I don't know if I would ever have been able to appreciate how amazing the good things in my life were if I hadn't known so much pain. I appreciated my life in a way I never thought possible. I was grateful for everyday tasks that most people take for granted. I enjoyed taking Vincent and Vance to the grocery store as much as I would if we had been at the park. I found joy in everything we did. Finding the Pride program was my first miracle. Getting to adopt Vincent and Vance was another miracle.

Part 2

Chapter 23
Call Me Papá

There are decisions that you make that change your life's trajectory and, often, the lives of others. Sometimes you may not have the slightest idea of the magnitude of a decision you have made until months, years, or maybe decades later. You look back and realize how consequential that one decision was. Essentially, it's the butterfly effect—a butterfly flaps its wings in Brazil to start a chain reaction that leads to a rainstorm in the Sahara. When you look back with the knowledge of all the things that would follow from that decision, would you decide differently? Knowing what you know now, would you have said yes instead of no or vice versa?

There are also choices you make, and you look back in hindsight and say to yourself, "If I could only do that over again…" Some decisions I would definitely make the same. Some I really wish I could do over. The decisions that I would come to make in the next few years would profoundly change the trajectory of my life, the lives of those around me, and the lives of the generations who would follow us. Unfortunately, these were not always for the best.

Six years had passed since Vincent and Vance made me a father. I was no longer afraid of getting fired at work every day, and the self-consciousness of my residual brain damage had subsided. My only real reminder of what had happened to me seventeen years earlier on Interstate 80 in Omaha, Nebraska, was the myoclonic seizure disorder that still popped up at inopportune times. When I would have an episode, Vincent and Vance had begun to copy my jerking movements and noise. It was actually hilarious and endearing to watch them copy the funny jerks and grunts I still had on occasion. I was doing well at work, and Apogee Food Company had recently relocated us to New Jersey from Chicago.

After Biri had left, I hadn't had very good luck dating. I had thought a few times that I had met a great guy only to discover that I was really bad at choosing boyfriends. I didn't want to be that cliché single parent who had a string of boyfriends whose kids called Papa. One boyfriend turned out to be a stalker and would just show up at my job and our condo after breaking up.

One boyfriend, whom I had for a year, actually went so wrong at the end; he faked his own death to get out of the relationship. I don't know if he didn't like me, the kids, or the responsibility of having an "instant family." He had walked out of our apartment one evening after putting the boys to bed. He left without his keys, his phone, or any other belongings. He left all his clothes and personal items behind. He simply walked out the door and didn't take his car. He was missing for fourteen days when I got a letter in the mail from Seattle saying he was going to kill himself. I had been crying for fourteen days straight and talked on the phone with his parents and friends looking for him, trying to figure out what had happened. A week after getting his letter in the mail, he turned up alive at a friend's house. I knew then that I was really bad at picking boyfriends and understanding how my relationships were going. I never saw *that* coming.

I had met Joseph on a dating website just before the boys turned six. We moved in together shortly after meeting. This was a bit quick, but we were both about forty years old, and sometimes you just have to make a decision and make things work. To find a proper coparent for my kids, I approached finding a partner like a business objective. My regular dating ideas hadn't worked, so I had to think differently. There were not very many gay men who were in my age range who also wanted kids.

More than half the gay men my age died in the 1980s and 1990s from AIDS. I was now forty-something. There were so many more gay men fifteen years or younger than me that had no idea how badly AIDS had decimated our community, and they didn't need to. These young men were all also not in my consideration set. I decided that I needed to cast a wide net and did one hundred dates in one hundred days. I know this sounds exaggerated, but I was a bit desperate.

I was on a mission to find a new boyfriend and coparent for my sons. I did coffee dates, dinner dates, and lunches with a hundred men who responded to my dating profile. Being a single gay dad on a dating website was not very common and apparently was not very desirable. Most of my dates ended after a very short interaction. I realize that many dating apps are more about hooking up than actually dating. This became clear as I went through my list of potential "future husband" candidates. I had second dates with five guys and then had a third date with three that included Vincent and Vance. My plan was to screen the candidates, but Vincent and Vance were going to choose their new "other dad" from the three who made it through to the end.

Candidate number 1 was a high school gym teacher and football coach. He was ten years older than me with blond hair, blue eyes, and very fit physique. He was excited at the prospect of having sons to play sports with. Candidate number 2 was my first choice. He was of Puerto Rican descent and had parents who were in their eighties. His parents had him very late in life, so he lived and took care of them. Family was very important to him. He did similar work to what I did and was a little chubby. He was endearing and clumsy. Our family date consisted of going for a hike in the woods. He tripped at one point on the trail and rolled down a hill. He was fine and he tried really hard to make a good impression. Then there was Joseph, candidate number 3.

I knew Vincent and Vance were going to pick Joseph from the moment they met him. Our family date with Joseph consisted of taking the boys to the Brookfield zoo. I didn't want the boys to know I was dating anyone, and I thought the zoo would be a good opportunity to see how Joseph interacted with the boys. Vincent and Vance were sitting in their car seats in the second row of our minivan when we pulled up to get Joseph. Joseph got in our minivan and looked back at the boys in their car seats and introduced himself.

"Hello, Vance and Vincent, I am Mr. Joseph." Joseph was tall and dressed very professionally. He carried an expensive-looking handbag and wore shoes that did not look the least bit comfortable. He had a fresh haircut with a fade and trimmed sideburns. Joseph wore designer glasses with very thick lenses that made his eyes look small. The boys both said, "Hello," but were suspiciously quiet as we drove toward the zoo. I could see that they were staring at Joseph in the rearview mirror.

The Vance spoke up. "Mr. Joseph, do you have a girlfriend?" he asked.

"No," replied Joseph. I looked at him, somewhat embarrassed.

The boys sat quietly for a few minutes, and then Vance asked again, "Mr. Joseph, do you have a boyfriend?"

"No," replied Joseph again.

I was getting more embarrassed at where the conversation was heading when Vance quickly followed up with, "Do you *want* a boyfriend?"

I knew at that moment that I had found someone who wanted to raise kids and have a family as much as I did, and the boys had chosen Joseph. It was love at first sight. Vincent and Vance had made their choice. I was Dad, and Joseph was going to be Papá. Papá was pronounced the same way children would in France or Spain with the accent on the second syllable. Joseph had lived in both Spain and France and knew that he wanted to be called Papá if and when he had children.

We had all lived in Joseph's condominium in the Andersonville neighborhood of Chicago for the last three years when my job had only given us six weeks to relocate to New Jersey after I accepted the new role. Joseph had found a home to rent online, and movers took only one day to pack our three-bedroom condo for the move. We were now going to be a suburban family of four. I am forever amazed at the twists and turns in my life. Just ten years earlier, I was handicapped and living in an empty Section 8 apartment with Daryl in an impoverished part of Chicago. We had pulled a mattress and couch from a dumpster so that we had something to sleep on. I now had a huge moving van packed, ready to move us to a suburban house in one of the most affluent counties in the US with the family that I had created. Ten years earlier, I would have never, ever believed any of this was possible.

CHAPTER 24
Please Adopt Me

For the next two years, Joseph and I tried to have a biological child through in vitro fertilization and a surrogate. The egg donor was of Polish descent like I was. This baby would have been the closest to what an actual baby would look like if Joseph and I could have had a biological child. The process did not go well and took a toll on Joseph. Sometimes it is hard to admit how much you really want something to happen. You may really want something in your life, something that makes you happy, gives you peace, and truly fulfills you. When you open that door to really wanting that thing, you are also opening the door to the possibility of being hurt and disappointed.

I don't know how long Joseph had wanted children, but becoming Vincent and Vance's Papá fully opened his door for wanting more, including a daughter. He dreamed of having a daughter and doing all the things a dad would do with their daughters. The process he went through to conceive a baby was frustrating and cost him a large sum of money. He had been disappointed by the process and the people whom he had thought he could trust and depend on. I knew there were times he would sit in the bathroom, frustrated and disappointed, and cry to himself.

Even as a gay man, Joseph had some strong stereotypical male tendencies, like never letting anyone see him cry or his vulnerabilities. He had saved the money he needed to have a biological child over several years, and now that money was mostly gone, yet there was no baby on the way. The process of having a baby using in vitro fertilization with an egg donor and surrogate was expensive. Through some misfortunes and misaligned trusts, the money was spent with no prospect for a baby.

I felt bad for Joseph. I could see his dream of becoming a biological parent get crushed, even though he wouldn't say anything. I think the reason he didn't want to say too much about not having his baby was so Vincent and Vance wouldn't think they weren't good enough. I had adopted Vincent and Vance through the foster care system. So I suggested to Joseph that we adopt a daughter through New Jersey foster care to round out our family instead. We were a family of four with no girls. I could see that after suggesting adoption, Joseph had to go through a period of mourning the loss of not having a biological child. After some time, he agreed. Joseph and I had now decided that we wanted to grow our family and adopt a daughter, a girl who would be younger than Vincent and Vance. This one decision to adopt a daughter would have consequences that reached much further. It would start a chain reaction of other decisions that would profoundly change our lives and ultimately the lives of many others.

Our new life in New Jersey was going well. The kids were in a good elementary school, my new position was going well at work, and having a backyard was a great change. I hadn't lived anywhere with a yard since my car accident seventeen years earlier. I had always wanted a vegetable garden, so I bought a rototiller and dug up a large patch in the middle of the backyard. We got a blow-up swimming pool for the boys to play in, along with other yard toys and games. We also got a gas grill and put it in the backyard. We were all enjoying spending time together outside.

Joseph had dreamed of having a daughter and was enjoying preparing a bedroom for our soon-to-be daughter, whoever she was. He painted the bedroom yellow and bought a white sleigh bed with a matching dresser. He even bought pillows, sheets, and a comforter to go with it.

We had finished thirteen weeks of foster parent classes and had done all the interviews and home inspections. Only a few weeks had gone by when we got a call. We were elated when we were told a si-year-old girl named Stacey would be available for adoption. They also told us that she had an eight-year-old sister named Kareela, if we were interested in adopting two girls instead of one. The foster care system will always figure out how to place as many kids with a family as possible. To the system, foster kids are like potato chips; you can't take just one. However, we wouldn't be able to meet them in person for a few weeks. They were both younger than Vincent and Vance, who were now nine. This was really going to happen! We were going to be dads to daughters!

I was finishing work one afternoon just before a four-day weekend for the Fourth of July holiday when I received a phone call from our social worker, who was helping us with the adoption of our daughters. "Hello," said the social worker, "we have a situation here at our office."

Okay, that didn't sound good, and anything that would impact our adoption was more than I wanted to hear.

"You and Joseph are planning to adopt Kareela and Stacey, right?" she asked rhetorically. "We have their brother here at our office right now. His foster mother just dropped him off here because she says that she is going on vacation for the Fourth of July and can't take him with her."

We didn't know there was a brother, and I was bothered by the fact that a foster parent would just drop off a child at a foster care center. The social worker continued, "Since he is their brother, you will eventually meet him. Would you be able to take him as a temporary placement for the four-day weekend?"

Let me pause here in this story. As I have mentioned, some moments and questions transform your life. I didn't know how much this simple question would change the trajectory of ours.

"Could you take him for the four-day weekend?" she asked again. This is a simple question. It's a weekend. This is a twelve-year-old boy for a weekend. A boy who will be, at least tangentially, in our lives, anyway. Why wouldn't we say yes?

Without giving it much thought, I told her that we would take the brother for the weekend, of course. We hadn't even met Stacey and Kareela, but Joseph and I were both excited to get some idea of what they would be like from meeting their brother, whose name was D'andre.

I arrived at the foster care center and was met by our social worker and brought to a visitation room. D'andre was a very small boy for being twelve years old and had a reddish-brown afro with front teeth that stuck out parallel to the ground. He had a goofy grin on his face and wouldn't look at me directly. He had a backpack and a light jacket. When I walked up, he was sitting on a folding chair, holding his backpack on his lap with his head down. D'andre had been in two different foster homes with his sisters and then was placed in two foster homes by himself. The most recent was with an older woman who was a retired schoolteacher. D'andre had already been in foster care for more than two years.

D'andre timidly asked if I had any kids, and I showed him pictures of Vincent and Vance on my phone. He had no idea we were planning to adopt his sisters, and I was told not to say anything. I could tell from the moment I met him that something was off. He seemed timid and scared, more scared and timid than I thought he would be as a kid in foster care. I assumed it was because he had suffered some kind of significant trauma in his short life, something worse than most kids who were in foster care. When your soul has been damaged and you have suffered immense pain, you can sense it in others. There is a look or the way a person holds themselves that only other people who have also experienced trauma and loss can identify and understand. Vincent and Vance had suffered some neglect, but the impact of that neglect had been mostly erased by consistent and constant love and attention. Vincent and Vance weren't yet three when I got them. This boy was twelve, and my heart immediately went out to him from sensing the pain in his soul. I told the social worker we would take him home for the holiday weekend, and D'andre agreed.

As I led him to the elevator, he shirked as if in pain. "I-I-I can't get in there," he said.

"Okay then, we'll go down the steps," I replied and tried to comfort him. I opened the door to the large cavernous stairwell, and D'andre held on tightly to the rail and slowly went down each step, carefully, one at a time. This child was severely traumatized by having to go down steps or get into an elevator. The social worker did not give me any heads-up that this child was so traumatized. Did she know? Was D'andre exaggerating? Did the social worker just not want to tell us?

On the drive to our home, D'andre didn't say much. He told me about the older woman who was his foster mom and that he liked to ride his bike and play basketball. This seemed like a good thing, as Vincent and Vance also liked to ride their bikes and play basketball.

When we got home, it was close to dinnertime. I introduced D'andre to everyone, and the twins took D'andre upstairs to show him their bedroom where he would be staying for the long weekend. The boys played in the driveway for a while. At dinner, we could see that D'andre did not eat anything. He pushed his food around his plate. He then started to quietly cry.

"What's the matter, D'andre?" Joseph said. We could all see that this boy was experiencing some significant emotional pain.

"Will you adopt me?" he blurted out. "You…you have kids, I've wanted to have brothers…will…will you adopt me?"

We all sat a bit dumbfounded. We had just met D'andre a few hours earlier.

His plea was heartbreaking, and all of us began to get emotional. Suddenly, D'andre got up from his chair and walked out the front door. I quickly followed him down the block and stopped him. He fell to the ground in our neighbor's driveway and started crying. I knelt down, wrapped my arms around D'andre, and held him as he cried. We rocked back and forth, sitting crooked on the sidewalk. I could feel every bit of his pain. His tears soaked through the front of my shirt.

Rocking the soul-damaged boy back and forth, trying to comfort him, transformed me back to a time when I was damaged, hurt, and alone. I remembered lying in bed for two years, confused and profoundly lonely. I remembered wanting to die when Stuart kicked me out of my home. He was the only person I knew and could remember at that time. I remembered relapsing at my psych halfway house in Chicago. Every bit of pain I had to endure to get to where I was today had to mean something. Some good had to come from it. My suffering had to mean *something*.

I could feel this boy's pain as if it was my own. What could have happened to a twelve-year-old boy to make him behave like this? If I could help someone through their pain, I had to do it. There had to be some reason for me to recover from so much trauma, so much pain, and so much sadness. Right there and then, I knew we *had to* adopt D'andre and we had to help him recover from whatever trauma he had gone through. There was really no other option. I couldn't *not* be there for him. There had to be some good that came from the suffering I endured for so many years. I believed right then and there that the purpose was to help others on their journey to recovering from their trauma, starting with D'andre.

I had no idea what had happened to this child, but I held him tightly, putting one hand on the back of his head and the other around his back. I pulled him close and rocked him slowly back and forth like a baby. "I was alone and hurting, too, when I was younger," I told him. "I know how you feel. Yes, we can adopt you, D'andre." I said yes, even though I had no idea if it was possible and hadn't discussed it with Joseph.

This decision to have D'andre come stay with us for the weekend and then telling him that we would adopt him had a profound impact on how I saw myself, my reason to be, and the reason I had to suffer so much pain and trauma in my life. I could feel so much of what this boy was feeling. His soul was profoundly hurt and scarred. I knew I had to do something to make things better. I was changed as a person from first experiencing profound loss and pain and then from recovering from it to have a decent and happy life. I was also changed from meeting D'andre and realizing that there weren't very many people who could help him or even want to help him. I knew we had to try.

CHAPTER 25
Dads of Daughters

Being a dad of daughters is much different than being a dad of sons. Joseph had always wanted girls. He wanted to do their hair, go shopping, and all the stuff that many girls enjoy. We met Kareela and Stacey two weeks after I told D'andre we would adopt him. D'andre didn't know until the day his sisters showed up at our home with their social worker that we had already planned to adopt his sisters. They appeared to be sweet, lovely little girls and arrived with their suitcases in tow. They each had their hair done in braids with beads at the ends of each one that would make clicking sounds as they turned their heads.

We brought them to their room and showed them their new home. Stacey and Kareela were excited to see their brother, and he was very happy to see them too. They each chose a bed and began to get settled into their new forever home. Within a short time, they had unpacked their little suitcases and had taken out all of the toys we had stocked in their room. On their first day in our home, the first day that Joseph and I would be the parents of five children, I sat all five of the children next to each other on a bed and took a picture. I kept this photo on my desk at work as a reminder of the hopes and dreams we had for our children. It was a reminder of why I go to work each day and tried my best. They were all in pajamas and smiling—all so young with so much potential.

I don't remember the impetus for the first time Joseph and I realized the absolute gravity of issues that our new daughters had. Still, I remember clearly what the outcome was. D'andre had come to us a broken and damaged child, and so did his sisters. Kareela and Stacey were eight and six, respectively, but both had birthdays in the next few months and were soon to be nine and seven. They had brought some toys with them when they moved in with us, but we had also bought them many new dolls and games and art supplies. Again, I don't remember what caused this first incident, but it was only the first of many.

The girls had moved in with us just a few days earlier. I was cooking dinner in the kitchen when I heard Kareela start screaming in the living room. Not playful screaming, not angry screaming, but terrified shrieking. Then Stacey started shrieking as if in horrifying pain. Joseph and I both ran to them to find the girls screeching, kneeling on the floor, pulling at their hair. They both had their hands clenched in fists that they thrashed in the air and then would hit themselves in the head or on their chest. Joseph and I were panicked and dumbfounded as we scanned the room, trying to identify the cause of this commotion. We could find nothing.

Joseph picked up Stacey like a ragdoll and inspected her, "What's wrong?" he repeatedly yelled, trying to be heard over the screeching of our new daughters. We tried to question them, calm them, and even tried to distract them.

"Are you hurt?" we yelled to be heard over the screaming. We could find nothing. The screaming and crying continued for more than two hours this first time, and Joseph and I sat down to try to even conceptualize what had happened to these girls to cause this behavior.

Children can't usually tell you what is hurting them; they don't have the words. However, their behaviors and reactions will reflect how they feel inside. Our new children's emotional pain would manifest itself in many different ways as we would come to learn. The girls shrieked and screamed for hours. It was horrifying to listen to them for up to four hours straight without stopping. This was not normal at all, and it was definitely not okay. We had met other kids in foster care over the years. We had friends who had adopted kids from foster care. No one's kids had episodes like we were experiencing with the girls. Something had happened to these girls, and no one knew what that was. The social workers and therapists that the girls had gave us no indication that this type of behavior happened. We had no idea what we had signed up for. What had happened to these kids? We had no clue from the adoption agency. There was not even a hint. We had been told that they were removed from their parents for neglect and abuse. That someone had reported the family to New Jersey Family Services, and the kids had been found in their apartment without lights, food, or any adult supervision. That's really all that was said.

These girls had been in foster care for more than two years and had been taken from their parents' home at four and six years old. What had happened at such a young age to make them react this way more than two years later? Had their parents done something? What had they seen? Had something happened in foster care? Did a former foster parent do something to them? Every parent has a moment when they ask themselves, "Can we do this? Can I do this? Do I even *want* to do this?" It would take years to find out what truly happened to these children and to fully understand the lasting impact it would leave.

Even without knowing the truth of the trauma these children endured, Joseph questioned whether or not we could parent these children. Our home was their fifth foster placement in two years. This meant that four other families decided they could not continue parenting these kids. The girls had been separated from their brother, and we found that there was still one more sister in a different foster home and at least four other half siblings. I knew what it was like to feel discarded and unimportant. I knew what it was like to hurt and be afraid to let anyone know that you are hurting. I knew that these children were not going to find another forever home; they were too damaged. What had happened to them?

D'andre, Kareela, and Stacey were beautiful but sad. You could see it in their faces and their actions. The first time I went to hug Kareela, she just stood there limp, not moving. They had moments where they acted like perfectly normal children. Then there were obvious signs of trauma. Then there were horrendous moments like now when the girls would shriek and pull at their hair for no obvious reason, screaming at the top of their lungs for many hours at a time.

Everything I had gone through until now told me I was meant to parent these children and that the universe brought them into our lives for a reason. I had been dependent on others when I was handicapped and was abandoned by Stuart, the only person I knew at the time. I knew how it felt to be betrayed by the person who was supposed to take care of you.

I knew that this was not the experience that Joseph had anticipated when we decided to adopt "a daughter." Joseph was raised in a "normal" home and had a "normal" upbringing. He was looking forward to having a "normal" family and do "normal" family stuff. My "crazy" was oftentimes more than he could stand. I knew that we were meant to be parents to these children. No matter how hard this was going to be, I knew there were not very many people who could parent these children or even want to try. It was a miracle that we all found each other. These children needed someone who could show them what "normal" was, and that was Joseph. I had no idea what a normal family was supposed to be like. I did not remember most of growing up. I had no point of reference. For all intents and purposes, I was raised in a psychiatric halfway house in Chicago, which was not "normal." This was where my historical memory started. These kids also needed someone who could unconditionally accept all the craziness that was to come and help them through it. They needed to believe that someone understood them. Feeling like no one can understand you is an awful feeling. Having a parent who could completely relate to their trauma, whatever that trauma was, could be just what they needed.

CHAPTER 26
Front Steps

I don't know what I had for expectations of all five kids getting along together. I was probably living in a bit of a fantasy land, thinking that all the kids would somehow magically blend together. I saw our family as more like the Brady Bunch than what the reality was. The first Halloween we were all together, we made our annual pilgrimage to a pumpkin farm to get pumpkins, ride carnival rides, take a hayride, and go through the corn maze. Halloween pumpkin patch festivities had become a tradition since adopting Vincent and Vance seven years earlier. This was our first family outing as a family of seven.

The fall day couldn't have been more beautiful. The weather was cool, but it was sunny. Our minivan fit everyone, and we started out on the hour-long car ride to the pumpkin farm. We had the expected seat kicking and complaining about who got to sit in which seat. The pumpkin farm sat in a valley between low peaks covered with maple trees in full fall color. Vincent and Vance loved carnival rides—bumper cars, Ferris wheels, and all the spinning twisting rides. The girls didn't really want to ride any of the carnival rides once we got there, and D'andre was afraid to get on many of them. There was bickering and pouting, but that was normal kid stuff that parents deal with every day.

Then we got to the corn maze. The corn maze covered an acre or two. It was pretty large and set off to the back edge of the pumpkin farm. We were told that it can take sixty to ninety minutes to get through the corn maze before we headed in. It sounded fun; a cool, sunny fall day, holiday festivities, what could go wrong?

We all started in the corn maze looking for our first of many clues to the corn maze puzzle. We were deep in the tall cornfield when D'andre began to get agitated and angry, but I was trying to keep him calm. Something made him really angry, something minor and stupid like not getting to carry the corn maze map. He puffed up his chest, yelled in the middle of the corn maze, and then disappeared through the rows of corn in a rage, crying and yelling. He threatened to hit his siblings before running off and had started physically pushing them around, which set off all the other kids.

As I was lost in a giant corn maze with four screaming kids ranting about their brother who had threatened them, trying to find that angry, disturbed child, I realized our lives were profoundly changed. I wanted to hold on to the belief that this was a road bump and we could pull together. This was not to be reality.

That fantasy version of the perfect family I was desperately trying to hold on to was completely shattered one evening, shortly after the Halloween outing. I had walked into Vincent and Vance's bedroom to find Kareela and one of her brothers under a blanket on the floor, curled up together, kissing and fondling each other. What do you even say as a parent? Who could conceptualize this? Kareela immediately jumped up and ran to her own bedroom. What was happening?

Her brother said, "Dad Dad Dad Dad Dad, she kept trying to touch me." Kareela was still eight, so this was definitely not normal. "She…she…she kept coming up to me trying to kiss the back of my neck. She…she…she wouldn't leave me alone," he stuttered. I could see that the boy was very traumatized. What had we done bringing in these damaged kids to our home?

I walked over to the girls' bedroom. Kareela looked at me with a blank expression on her face. "What happened, young lady?" I asked her. She wouldn't talk and she wouldn't move. I reached down, picked up Kareela, and took her outside to the front step. It was dark outside, but we needed privacy for this conversation. With seven people in a relatively small house, outside was the only place we would get any privacy.

Kareela sat with a blank expression on her face. "What?" she asked. "What do you want?"

"I want to know what happened," I said.

"What?" she said expressionlessly with her mouth wide open, holding out her hands with her palms up. Her eyes looked dead and distant to the point of being disturbing.

"Your brother said you kept trying to touch him?"

Our fruitless conversation went on for an hour. She denied anything had happened. She flat out called me a liar and told me that I didn't see what I know I obviously saw.

"Kareela, how did you know to do this stuff?" I asked. "Has someone done this to you?" There was a long pause as we sat quietly on the front steps looking into the dark street. "Someone touched me inappropriately when I was a kid," I said in a low voice. "You can tell me anything. I get it." I thought back to the horror of being raped when I was thirteen, not being able to tell anyone and not able to fathom what had happened to Kareela.

"What if it was my father?" she said and looked me in the face for the first time during the entire conversation. But that was all she said that evening. I lied and told her everything was going to be okay and sent her back in the house. I sat quietly in the dark of the front steps, pondering the gravity of what just happened before going back inside. She would have been five or six years old. What had happened? How could—*why* would someone do that to a child?

CHAPTER 27
Here Comes the Bride

A few weeks before becoming parents to five children in 2013, the US Supreme Court struck down DOMA, the Defense of Marriage Act, allowing for federal recognition of same-sex marriages. While sitting at a fun-plex during our twin's ninth birthday party with all of their friends and their friend's parents, I had asked Joseph to marry me in the least romantic way possible. I suggested that since it was now legal for us to get married, we should do it because of the tax and insurance benefits. He said yes.

We had been together for four years, and neither of us was going anywhere. We did not always get along as a couple, but we were both very dedicated to raising our kids and having a family. Both of us viewed raising children more as a vocation or calling, and we both knew we couldn't do it on our own. Finding someone who shares your life's passion is rare. Being able to marry them and have their complete support in fulfilling your life's passion is even rarer.

We had planned a small wedding with a few friends and a few of my family members. Joseph had a large extended family, but like most of the gay men I had been with in my rehabilitation program, his family didn't accept him. I believe this is one of the reasons that Joseph so badly wanted to create a family of his own.

A few days before we told the kids we were getting married, D'andre had asked me why I didn't want my own bedroom since everyone wants their own room. I wondered if D'andre realized we were gay. He was twelve, but maybe he didn't know anyone who was gay before. Did he think we were just roommates? I asked Joseph if he thought D'andre knew we were gay. Joseph said he was probably pulling my leg and looked at me like I was dense. Indeed, I fell for it.

When I asked D'andre if he knew what Papá and I were to each other, he said, "Yes, you guys are gay." Then he smiled and laughed, knowing that he had gotten one over on his new dad.

*****

Our three new kids had lived with us only four months when an event so disturbing happened that I truly wondered if we were equipped to manage what was happening. Sometimes desire is not enough. Wanting to help and being able to help are two completely different things. I knew we wanted to make these kids' lives better, but this event made me question if we actually could. It was just two days before Joseph and I were going to be married at Christ Episcopal Church. We had done our marriage counseling with the minister and had gotten matching black tuxedos for Vincent, Vance, D'andre, and ourselves. We had gotten black and white dresses for Kareela and Stacey that matched the tuxedos.

D'andre came to me very concerned and had me come into his bedroom. He was obviously distressed. "Shhh, stay quiet," he said. D'andre directed me to sit on his bed close to him. "Papá is cheating on you with the lady down the street!" he exaggerated while still trying to speak quietly. His eyes were big, and he was acting very afraid. He was breathing very hard, and I was afraid he was going to hyperventilate. He continued in a loud whisper, "I wanted to tell you, but he said he would kill me if I said anything! He took a big knife and put it up on my neck."

"D'andre," I said in a calm voice, "Papá is not cheating on me with the lady down the street."

"He is! He is! I saw him! And you're too much of a stupid bitch to know. He said he was going to kill me!" *Okay, what in the heck is happening here? This is unreal.* "And Papá has been hitting me with a belt, and you don't care!" D'andre said, shaking and crying.

This line of conversation went on for an hour. What was happening? He tried to show me marks on his arms where Papá had hit him with this imagined belt. D'andre was obviously reenacting a scene from his prior life with his parents. How does this happen? D'andre believed that I was his mom and Papá was his dad. Holy Mother of God, what was happening? Our three new children all displayed the most extreme post-traumatic behaviors.

We called the foster care helpline to report what was happening and tell them we needed help with D'andre. Instead of helping, we had two social workers come over to investigate us for abuse the next day. This was the day before our wedding with a house full of guests. The social workers took each of the kids into a room by themselves, interviewed them, and then interviewed each of us. They were in our home for five hours; it was infuriating, but there was nothing we could do. It was a surreal experience.

We explained that our soon-to-be-adopted son had been reliving scenes from his past, believing that I was his mother and Papá was his father. I don't know if these social workers had any idea how seriously disturbed our son was or if they thought we were hiding something from them. We realized early in the process of adopting our kids that the foster care system was not set up to help kids as much as it was to protect themselves from litigation.

By the next day, D'andre had snapped back into reality. I sat talking with him for a long time. It took a lot of questions and clarification, but the reality of the story was so much worse than Joseph or I could have ever thought. This is the story I was finally able to piece together. D'andre told me that his father would beat his mother with an aluminum bat, and she would just take it. He had never told anyone. He said that his father would hit him all the time for almost any reason. If he was reading aloud and pronounced a word wrong, his father would slam his face into the table. For not cleaning the bathroom right, his father had pulled him out of bed in the middle of the night, threw him in the shower, beat him with a leather belt, and then made him sleep on the concrete basement floor still wet. His father would push him downstairs, which explained why D'andre had been so afraid of going down the stairwell that first day I met him at the adoption agency. D'andre's dad was extremely abusive both physically and psychologically.

The worst for D'andre came out over the next two days as he continued to open up and talk more about the things that had happened to him when he lived with his parents. I knew how hard it was to trust someone enough to tell them about something really bad that happened. I had kept my own secret about being raped when I was thirteen for many years. I cannot imagine the strength a child must have to trust someone and tell them this story. D'andre was only twelve and had now been in foster care for two years. It had been at least two years since any of this happened, and he hadn't told anyone. The worst was still to come out. The kids had three older sisters. Two of them were half sisters from Jamaica who had moved to the US and moved in with them all.

I sat in disbelief, as the incredible reality was too much for me to conceptualize. D'andre went on to tell me that he was six when he saw his father raping his older half sisters. D'andre would wake up to use the bathroom and see his father having sex with his sisters in the living room. For a child to be exposed to this at such a young age leaves an indelible scar. As D'andre grew older, his father became more brazen and would rape his older half sisters in the living room while he was playing video games. His father would dare him to turn around and say anything about it. This was beyond my ability to conceptualize. This man was a monster. We know he didn't drink or use drugs; he was simply evil. Not that drugs or alcohol can excuse anything, but he was able to perpetrate all this evilness sober. *That* is a *special* kind of evil.

Against the foster care system's advice, we took D'andre to the county prosecutor's office the next day. He was able to tell the prosecutor the whole story. D'andre's father was arrested and put in jail that day. We discovered that one of his half sisters, who had been repeatedly raped, had gone to the police and reported the crime several years earlier. She tried unsuccessfully to have charges pressed against him. Without corroboration, charges weren't pressed. The father claimed the two were "dating." Okay, I really could not understand how this man had not been arrested before this. With D'andre's bravery, his father was arrested and was not able to post bail. He was later convicted and sentenced to serve six years in jail.

Several days after this amazing act of bravery, our D'andre had a complete psychological meltdown. D'andre tried to strangle his siblings, threatened to kill himself, smashed holes in the walls of his bedroom, and smashed anything breakable. He fell apart. D'andre had made the first step in recovering from such a horrid ordeal by naming the evil and calling it out. Admitting to God and the world that something really fricking bad happened and that it was not right or okay was a huge burden. *He* was *not* okay. Damn this horrible world that would allow such depravity to feast on the soul of an innocent child. Sexual abuse is the worst type of abuse for a child to endure, and when it is incest, it makes it so much more unbelievable and horrid.

I went to work the next day, sat in my car in the parking lot, and sobbed. I sat for thirty minutes in my car, trying to understand the horrors that I had learned of. We now knew what happened to D'andre, but we did not know the full extent of what happened to Stacey and Kareela. D'andre said that he never saw his younger sisters get raped or molested. This doesn't mean it didn't happen; he just wasn't forced to witness it.

As this event was unfolding, Joseph and I were married at Christ Episcopal Church in a small service with our friends and family members. Vincent, Vance, and D'andre were the ring bearers, and Stacey and Kareela were our flower girls. Never had I ever thought I would actually get married, and I never thought I would be a father to five children. Both are miraculous blessings. I also had never envisioned my wedding being accompanied by a social services investigation and trips to the police station. It had now been twenty years since I lost my memory and became crippled in a car accident. I was always amazed at the twists and turns my life took. Our new son had trusted us enough to tell us he was hurting and *why* he was hurting. This was amazing. I loved our three new children more than anyone could ever comprehend.

CHAPTER 28
It Only Gets Worse

Stacey, Kareela, and D'andre each had their own set of therapists and therapies. Every day, we had someone come to our home to provide some therapeutic service for our children, or we had to bring them somewhere for therapy. Literally every single day for a year, someone would come to our home to provide some therapeutic service for our kids; it was really too much and not enough.

Some of the therapists really were of no service at all. Many of the service providers for D'andre were actually afraid of him. One "doctor" met with D'andre each week for an hour, only to play basketball or let him sit and say nothing. This had gone on for a year.

Joseph asked the "doctor" if he could participate in D'andre's therapy sessions. When Joseph asked D'andre a provocative question to get him to talk, the "doctor" told Joseph that D'andre wasn't ready.

"It's been a year," said Joseph. "He has you fooled."

Another therapist would sit and wait for D'andre to "finish the next level of his video game" before she would start trying to talk to him. She had waited for twenty minutes of a forty-five-minute therapy session when Joseph intervened and told her that the video game didn't have levels. We finally had one miracle-working therapist who was able to get D'andre to talk. She was smart, tall, and didn't take any excuses. I cannot believe how many of D'andre's therapists were afraid of him. Any therapist who was afraid of D'andre needed to admit this and admit they could not help him instead of wasting time and wasting the opportunity for some other therapist to actually help.

During the first few years of having our three new children, Joseph was still working as a wedding and event coordinator. There were mornings he would need to head out early, and I would need to do the girls' hair. We could tell that our daughter Kareela was suffering on the inside and the outside.

She had started fourth grade just across the street from our house. Two girls whom she had befriended started teasing her for having gay dads.

"It's disgusting. Two dads. They're disgusting. You're disgusting," they would say.

We know that this had to be coming from the girls' parents. Up to this point, Vincent and Vance never had any issues with kids teasing them at school for having gay dads, but I had been bracing myself for this. Joseph and I were the first out, two-dad family in our town. Kareela had just moved into her fifth home in two years, had switched schools, had two new parents, and the girls at school who were supposed to be her friends were now picking on her.

It is an awful feeling when your kids hurt. It's worse when they hurt because of you. I had been waiting for this moment, and now it was here.

I told her, "Kareela, kids can pick on you for anything if they know it bothers you. It could be because your parents are fat, old, White, or gay. Or all of the above. It could be because you are a girl or because you're Black or anything." I had planned this speech for years, and this was the only incident where I had to use it. This was the only incident where any of our children told us they had been teased for having two dads. I was frankly surprised. Pleasantly surprised.

Kareela showed many signs that she was hurting inside. She would literally ask to go the nurse's office at school five, six, and seven times a day.

"My stomach hurts, my head hurts," she would say. One time, she started patting the air, pretending she couldn't see. She had lost chunks of hair from her head with large patches of some type of fungal infection. She literally had bloody wounds on the top of her head from stress. The fungal infections caused lesions and layers of scabs to form in her hair. Her internal stress caused Kareela to pick up every type of opportunistic skin disease. We had scabies and ringworm more times than I can bear to admit. It would then spread to the other kids and myself. Joseph very rarely got any of the skin problems.

We needed to get our kids better quality therapy and counseling. I had stepped into my daughter's room one day to find a color crayon drawing of a black and red stick figure killing Papá with a knife. It was Stacey. There was blood on the knife with dripping blood and Papá's head on the ground. She wrote "DED" on the picture. When your seven-year-old daughter draws a color crayon picture of herself killing someone, there is a problem. These kids had lived in a hellish home environment.

One evening, Kareela had been screaming and pulling out chunks of her hair. We had begun to get numb to the screaming and constant trauma being acted out. It's not that we didn't care. We had to become somewhat numb to endure it and not go craz, so we could *try* to get our kids the help they needed. Kareela had finally stopped and was spent from screaming and crying, so she went to her bed to lie down. Stacey, who was two years younger than Kareela, got a glass of water and a wet washrag and brought it to her and started patting Kareela's forehead with the wet cloth.

"What are you doing, Stacey?" asked Papá.

"I always do this," she said. What did it mean she always does this?

We found that Stacey and Kareela shared a room when they lived with their biological parents. Stacey explained that their dad would take her out of her own bed to the mother's room and have her sleep with her mom. He would then go back into the room with Kareela. After some time would pass, their dad would come back to get Stacey and carry her back into her own bedroom, where she would find Kareela shaking and crying quietly.

Stacey had learned at three and four years old how to comfort her sister after being molested or worse by their father. This meant that their mother was complicit in this horror show that they lived in. I could hardly believe what we had learned. We still didn't know what had happened to Kareela, but we had a pretty good idea, and it was heartbreaking. To know that our new kids' mother was complicit with all the abuse that had occurred with these children, *her* children, was incomprehensible. How could a mother who gave birth to these children allow them to suffer so much abuse? I realize their mother most likely had also been an abuse victim, but there has to be some line that gets crossed when it then happens to your kids. Joseph and I had been aware of other people who lost custody of their kids to foster care, but none of them was this depraved. How does a mother sit by and allow her five-year-old daughter to be molested or worse?

We had wanted a daughter. We got two and another son. These kids were incredibly damaged. Did we even know the extent of what really happened? What were the long-term effects of this damage? Could we simply love them enough to get them through it all? What about our originals, Vincent and Vance? How would they be impacted by the new kids?

*****

Right before Stacey, Kareela, and D'andre had come into our lives, I had planted a vegetable garden. New Jersey is nicknamed the Garden State because of its perfect climate and soil for growing a garden. I had always wanted to have a vegetable garden, so I had started tomato seeds inside in February. I moved twenty-five tomato plants outside into a garden that I had dug out of the lawn in May. By August, the tomato plants were each over seven feet tall and covered with blossoms and tiny green tomatoes. I had planted a variety of tomato plants—yellow tomatoes, large red tomatoes, striped heirloom tomatoes, etc. I had eight different varieties.

D'andre moved in with us July second, and the girls moved in August first. Over the next few weeks, as we came to understand the trauma and horrors these children endured, I forgot about my tomato plants and my garden. Each plant was covered with amazing tomatoes, and all of them rotted on the vine. There was no room to deal with anything other than the horrors that these children had faced. Our entire lives revolved around trying to help these children who had suffered more pain and trauma than a child, or anyone, should have to.

We researched doctors, therapists, treatments, and diagnoses. Our kids had experienced so much trauma early in life, and we didn't know what the long-term impact would be and if there was anything we could do now to make their lives better. Every day we had to believe we were doing the right thing and make the best decisions with the information we had at the time. We had to believe that the children would get better and that there was some hope for them to recover from all of this trauma. There had to be hope for happiness. Hope was all that we had and the only thing that allowed us to get through each day. You must have hope. Without hope, you have nothing.

CHAPTER 29
Noah

The adoption of Stacey, Kareela, and D'andre was finalized a few months after Joseph and I got married. Within the same year of adopting our three new kids, I was given a new position at work. I had worked now for eleven years since starting over from scratch, and I loved my job. The new position involved traveling to my company's offices around the world. I had never traveled outside of the United States except for going to Canada, and I was excited but nervous. With our now family of seven, we decided to buy a house. We had been renting a small home since moving to New Jersey.

Within a few months, Joseph and I had adopted three kids, gotten married, and were now going to buy a large home with seven bedrooms and four bathrooms. I got a new position at my job and, during the first year of it, traveled for work to eighteen different countries. That was amazing. Everywhere I went, I would buy T-shirts for the kids with the country I had visited on the front. I felt very guilty leaving Joseph at home for a week at a time with five children. I missed my kids deeply and would video-call each day so that I could see them.

On Halloween 2014, we moved into our own forever home. This is the house that we wanted each of our children to call home. Each child had their own room, and there was one extra room to spare. Shortly after moving into the house, we got a call from foster care. They had a boy in our town who was fourteen and needed a temporary placement while he worked out things with his parents. The boy was gay or transgender, and his parents didn't accept him was all we were told. While we thought this was a situation that we were ideal for helping with, we couldn't have foreseen what was to come from the decision to take him into our home. What was to follow was my biggest parenting failure and is my biggest regret since recovering from brain damage.

The first time we met Noah, the thing that stuck out to me the most was that he was very dramatic and loud. His mannerisms were very exaggerated, almost like a character in a theatrical production. His parents were immigrants. There had been long-term physical and psychological abuse in Noah's home. When his parents found out he was gay, that was bad. When he told them he was transgender, the parents had bought him a plane ticket to fly back to their home country so that the cousins could restore the family honor. We all believed this to mean that Noah was to be killed in an honor-killing by his relatives. This was such an extreme story, and we would find out later that everything about Noah was extreme. We were compelled to help him.

Noah was extraordinarily intelligent but had done poorly in school. He told us stories of physically fighting with his parents, running away, and living in abject poverty. Noah's father was an alcoholic and lost jobs as quickly as he could get them. I struggled to empathize with Noah, like I empathized with the other kids. Perhaps it was because he was so much like me, especially in the things that I didn't like about myself. He was moody, short-tempered, judgmental, and liked to be the center of attention.

While it had been a dozen years since I left the psychiatric halfway house in Chicago, I still had my own issues. I, too, was moody, short-tempered, judgmental, and liked to be the center of attention. Noah craved a lot of attention—all the attention—and would do things intentionally to get a reaction. Because this was very obvious and not healthy behavior, we told all the other kids to try to ignore some of Noah's attention-seeking antics.

The first time Noah put on a dress, we tried to be supportive and go about our normal business and not say anything. Apparently, Noah was trying to get a reaction because he went back to his room, changed clothes, and came out in girl's shorts and T-shirt, girl's boots, and had a stuffed bra. Again, we all went about our normal business and said nothing. Apparently, this was also not the reaction he wanted, so he went back into his room and came back out with girl's short shorts, an overstuffed bra, and excessive makeup. We still said nothing. After a few minutes, Noah stomped back into his room. He came back out a short time later with a clean face, sweatpants, and a regular old T-shirt. These were typical types of behaviors for Noah.

Noah was also a gay, maybe transgender, fourteen-year-old boy placed with two adult gay men. Noah craved attention and affection and was prone to exaggeration and imagination. We didn't want there to be any confusion about what was appropriate or not appropriate in our home. We were repeatedly investigated for many things that both well-meaning teachers and overzealous social workers had reported. Joseph and I put up ground rules about hugging for Noah. We told him we would give him "air hugs"; this meant we would put our arms around him without touching him. We would occasionally allow actual hugs, but only the top of our bodies had contact and only for the count of three.

We had done exactly what we believed social services had done wrong with our other kids. Put up things in place to mitigate legal liability, which was not necessarily right for the child. This ended up being our first of many mistakes with Noah. Noah craved a connection with people, and this was a barrier that we put in place. If I had to do it all over again, I would have hugged Noah as much as he needed and dealt with whatever social services investigation may have come from it. We were not off to a good start with Noah, and it was only going to get worse. Noah did not feel loved or wanted, and I was responsible for that.

CHAPTER 30
Riley

Vincent and Vance had ten half siblings. When we lived in Chicago, I made sure to get a photo of them with each of the ten. There were six on their biological mom's side and four on their biological dad's side. Riley shared the same biological mother as Vincent and Vance. He had lived with us in Chicago when he was eighteen years old. From the age of five to eighteen, Riley had been in fifty foster homes before coming to live with us. This might sound like an exaggeration, but indeed, it was true. This meant that Riley stayed for an average of three months in each foster placement over a thirteen-year period. The foster care system had failed Riley, and he was preparing to age out of the foster care system. So he needed somewhere to live.

During the last four years that we lived in Chicago, I had spent a lot of time with Riley and two other siblings of Vincent and Vance. All eight kids on their mother's side had been put up for adoption. One had been adopted at birth, one had been in prison since the age of fifteen, and one was a runaway. I would pick up the remaining three every couple of weekends and do something fun with them and their brothers. We would all go to the zoo, roller-skating, an arcade, or a movie. There were a lot of things to do with kids in Chicago.

While I wanted Vincent and Vance to have good memories of their brothers and sisters, I did a lot of this for me. I did not remember growing up or having a childhood. I still had long-term amnesia, and the first twenty-seven years of my life were mostly missing. What I did know was very cursory and not very good. Going out every couple of weekends for those few years with Vincent, Vance, and their three biological siblings gave me the childhood I didn't remember having. I believe that I had more fun than they did. I loved taking out all the kids to the different places around Chicago. I really looked forward to every outing.

Joseph's condo was only a block from the beach of Lake Michigan. In the summer, I would take out all five kids for the entire day, sit on the beach, and play in the sand and waves. When we were relocated to New Jersey, Riley was nineteen and decided he didn't want to leave Chicago, so he moved in with a friend. When we moved, I missed taking out Vincent and Vance's brothers and sister deeply. I may have been too indulgent with these kids and bought too many things for them. I may have spent too much time just having fun with them. While I gave them the gift of time as siblings together, they gave me the childhood that I never had, and I loved them for that.

We had been in the new house for a year when Riley called to tell us he was going to be a father. Riley was now twenty-four, his girlfriend was seventeen, and the baby was due in a few months, shortly after his girlfriend was to graduate from high school. He wanted them to have a fresh start and move his new family to New Jersey. While Joseph and I couldn't have been more excited about becoming grandparents, we knew that our son's plan had some issues.

I had loved Riley from early on when I got to meet and know all of Vincent and Vance's biological brothers and sisters. I could tell from the first time that I met him that he was damaged and had suffered traumas that no one his age should have suffered. I was childlike during the time that I was severely handicapped, and I had seen trauma and suffering through a child's eyes. Every time I met a child in foster care, my heart went out to them. I realize that my experiences led me to make emotional decisions, to have poor boundaries, and to have a "save the world" mentality. I get this, but this is who I was. I loved all of Vincent and Vance's biological brothers and sister the first time I met each of them. Riley had taken a special place in my soul. When Riley was thirteen, he was continuously moving from foster home to foster home. I asked social services if I could adopt him. I had already adopted his brothers. Each time, I was told that he was too difficult and wouldn't be a good influence on his little brothers. I was not allowed to adopt Riley. When Riley was fourteen, he suffered from extreme anorexia. The whites of his eyes were yellow, and his skin was ashy gray. I knew that he was suffering in silence. He would never say that anything wasn't okay. I know this is because he couldn't trust an adult.

When he came to live with us at eighteen, we asked him if we could adopt him. He told us that he was too old. Now at twenty-four years old with a baby, he asked Joseph and me if we would adopt him so that his child could have grandparents, and we did. Our grandson was born on June twentieth, our first grandchild. We adopted Riley a few months later to officially be his parents and to officially be grandparents. While we were already Daddy and Papá, we were now also Grampa and Pa Pa.

CHAPTER 31
Noah the Terrible, Daddy the More Terrible

While we made significant progress helping Noah get on track for school, we struggled to make any progress being his parents. My biggest regret being a parent was not knowing how to help Noah. Not just with the not knowing but also with *wanting* to help Noah. He could feel it. Noah was difficult and damaged. He lied, was manipulative, and could be incredibly mean to everyone in our home. He had an entitled attitude, and nothing we did or provided was good enough. Yet he was still just a child. A very damaged child who, I am sad to say, probably also became more damaged from the decisions I made and the things I did.

Noah came to our home as a "temporary placement" until he could sort things out with his parents. When social services would visit with Noah's father, the father would point-blank tell the social workers that he would kill Noah if he was returned. Social services asked us if we would adopt Noah since there was no real chance he was going to go back home.

I initially said, "No, we will not adopt Noah." This elicited a visit from the head of social services and multiple other caseworkers to our home to convince us that we *needed* to adopt Noah. Joseph supported my initial decision to not adopt Noah. I felt so guilty about not wanting to help or adopt Noah that I eventually agreed. Guilt is a strong force. It sounds counterintuitive, but that's what happened. Joseph also supported my decision to change my mind and have us adopt him. Joseph was much better with Noah than I was and had wanted to help Noah from the start.

Noah and I fought from the beginning. We would each try to one up each other and exert control. Noah was not going to be controlled, and if he was wronged, he would make sure to get revenge. We had many instances of Noah lying, stealing, or not following basic household rules. I had devised elaborate point schemes for assigning punishment. They never worked and only made things worse. Joseph and I researched tactics for parenting difficult children and researched various pediatric psychological conditions. Noah was an extreme child with extreme behaviors.

Noah would take no direction or feedback without retaliating, and there was really no line he wouldn't cross. I had asked Noah to clean a bathroom as part of his regular chores, like the chores the rest of the kids had. He didn't want to, so I grounded him. Noah reported us to child services, stating we were violating child labor laws. The social workers came out, investigated, and then told Noah he would have to follow the rules of the home. He didn't like that answer, so he reported the social workers on the child abuse hotline for not doing their job. The head of our county's social services department came to our home to meet with Noah to tell him to stop making false allegations and that he needed to follow the rules of our home. Noah didn't like that answer, so he started calling 911 when he would be asked to clean a bathroom. When he didn't get the response he wanted, he walked down to the police headquarters building to speak with a police supervisor. He would always take an issue further than anyone would ever think to.

Everything we tried made the situation worse until one day, Noah asked us to un-adopt him. Noah was only seventeen and legally could not be un-adopted or even emancipated. Once Noah decided not to have us as parents, he committed and did everything he could to make it happen. We had gotten a therapist for Noah, who told us that there was nothing she could do for Noah, as this was just how he was. She told us that she was really only coming for us to be able to endure Noah while he was still in our home. She also told us that Noah fanaticized about smashing in my head while I slept and that we needed to put measures in place to keep ourselves safe from Noah. She felt he was capable of inflicting physical damage or worse. Holy Mother of God, how did this go so wrong?

I woke up at two o'clock one morning to find Noah staring at me while I was sleeping. I was terrified. *Was he plotting to smash in my head while I slept?* I wondered. If you can't feel safe in your own home, there is a real problem. This happened two more times over the course of a few weeks. Whether Noah would have really hurt me is irrelevant. He didn't necessarily want to hurt me, but he wanted me to *believe* he could hurt me. He also alluded to poisoning the food and milk that was in our home. When Noah wanted something, there was no line he wouldn't cross to get what he wanted.

Within a few weeks of living in constant terror, I was hallucinating. I would see things happen, horrible things that weren't actually real. I saw a woman walking a dog by the park. Suddenly, I saw that dog lunge at two children walking by and bite them. I actually stopped my car and started yelling at her. "Your dog bit those kids!"

She looked at me in shock. "Sir, my dog did not bite anyone."

And it was true. Her dog had not bitten anyone. A few weeks later, I was going to the drugstore and saw a truck smash into a car with a bloody body thrown from the windshield. I stopped my car in the middle of the street to help, only to realize there was no car accident. There was nobody thrown from a car. How much stress do you have to be under to hallucinate really horrible things?

While Joseph and the other kids were stressed out by Noah, I was his chosen enemy and the barrier to getting what he wanted. We found that children or adults, like Noah, choose one victim at a time. I was in the bull's-eye. There was a time when Noah was so angry with me that as we were screaming at each other, I saw his eyes turn completely black. There was no white or brown…only black. Maybe I hallucinated it and maybe I didn't. His entire eyeballs turned black as we continued to scream at each other. I was convinced that I had seen the devil, and I was terrified.

Our entire world was imploding when I locked Noah out of the house one night for not following rules that he had agreed to. There was no line Noah wouldn't cross, so he called the police, and I was charged with child endangerment. Noah was removed from our home by social services, and I had to go in front of a judge to plead my case. If I was charged with child endangerment, I would have lost custody of all of our children. This was not happening.

The first day Noah was not in our home, I finally slept. A weight of terror had been lifted from our home. In court, I explained our circumstances to the judge. Thankfully, she understood, dismissed the charges, and provided services for Noah to get help.

I had made the decision to adopt Noah half-heartedly out of guilt, not love. This was the original sin. Everything else that transpired with Noah was a repercussion of that one decision. If you are going to raise a child, you must do it wholeheartedly. There must be nothing you wouldn't do for your child. If you can't love your child, then find someone who will—a grandparent, an aunt, an uncle, or a family friend. Find someone who can show that child love and then let them. A child must receive love; otherwise, they may develop into a monster. My fear and my shame were that I likely pushed Noah one step closer to becoming a monster. I could not love him for whatever reason. I shouldn't have tried to pretend that I did. It wasn't fair and it wasn't right. Noah taught us how not to raise a child, and I had to believe that this was the good that came from this situation. We were also forced to learn about pediatric psychological conditions, the effects of trauma on children, and about all the services and treatments for them. We had other challenging, damaged kids to raise. Hopefully, we would not make the same mistakes twice. I now understood that if you don't have love, you have nothing. I'm so very sorry, Noah. I hope you can forgive me one day.

CHAPTER 32
Bad Grampa

Riley and his new family arrived in New Jersey just a few days after the birth of their child, our first grandchild. He was so small and precious. I had gotten Vance and Vincent at two and a half, so I really had no experience with a newborn baby. We had gotten Riley and his new family an apartment in the town we lived in with all the needed furnishings for their one-bedroom apartment. We also got them a jeep so they could get back and forth to work and school. Riley was going to find work, and his girlfriend was going to start taking classes at the local community college. As new grandparents, we would watch our grandson while the new parents did what they needed to grow and support themselves and their family. While this all sounded great in theory, this is not what happened.

Riley had a tumultuous childhood with a lot of trauma that he never spoke of. We know this trauma had occurred from the sheer fact that he was in fifty different foster homes. That alone is a traumatic event for a child. We had become aware of various bits and pieces from foster care documents. Still, there were likely many things that happened to Riley that were never reported.

Riley had gotten a job at a printing shop, and his girlfriend had started school. Everything appeared to be going well when I got a call from Riley's landlord asking to meet with me in person. I was concerned and met with him at a coffeehouse later that day. The landlord told me that the other tenants in the building were complaining about all the fighting and screaming at all hours of the night coming from my son's apartment. They would hear yelling, loud thumps, and the baby crying. Apparently, the police had been called several times.

The landlord asked me if I could get the situation under control. When I heard all of this, I was simply beside myself with frustration. Why was my son fighting in the middle of the night with his girlfriend? Why did it escalate to the point that the police had to be called? They had only moved in a few months earlier. Was the honeymoon period over? Riley and his girlfriend hadn't lived together before since his girlfriend had just graduated from high school a few days before giving birth.

Joseph and I talked with our son about the complaint. Apparently, he was very angry with many things that his girlfriend was doing, and he didn't trust her. He believed she was cheating on him with virtually everyone and anyone. His girlfriend told us that Riley was a control freak and didn't allow her to have any friends, text, or call anyone. This seemed like a stereotypical case of an abusive, controlling boyfriend. Her explanation was believable, and our son's justification seemed exaggerated.

The fighting did not stop, and we blamed our son for everything. He was a man and, it appeared, the aggressor. Our son's girlfriend would take the baby and leave Riley for a few days or weeks at a time on several different occasions over the next few months and would come to live with us. Our son would fume with anger at everyone. He would even smash her phone or break her things. On one occasion, he poured an entire gallon of bleach in her basket of clean laundry. Ultimately, he would make up with his girlfriend, and she and our grandson would move back into the apartment with our son.

The fighting was escalating, and our son and his girlfriend were making more and more serious accusations and allegations against each other regarding things that affected their child. Riley told me to call social services to get involved because it had gotten to the point that he couldn't manage any longer. Our son's allegations against his girlfriend coupled with the ones she made against him were all severe enough that our grandson was in jeopardy of being placed in foster care.

Foster care can be a vicious cycle. A child is placed in foster care because of abuse and neglect. That child doesn't get the support they need to recover from the traumas that put them in foster care. Foster care itself can be a traumatic and negative experience for many. These children grow up with anger and trust issues, and then they have their own child. The untreated trauma causes the now parent to choose toxic relationships, have anger issues, and make poor parenting decisions. You can only parent like you were parented if there is no intervention.

We did not want to see our grandson placed in foster care. We could see that our son and his girlfriend had so many issues that it was very likely that they would permanently lose custody, and our grandson would be adopted by another family. Our son and his girlfriend were in many ways worse than the parents of our adopted children at the same stage of life. Our son and his girlfriend signed over custody of our grandson before he could be taken away and placed with another family.

After a few weeks, our son and his girlfriend expected us to sign our grandson back over to them since their case was closed with family services. They believed we were just playing some scam to get one over on the system. We were not. The court had set a list of conditions for our son and his girlfriend to get custody back that included therapy, parenting classes, and supervised visitation. Our son was furious with us, with me.

When we told Riley that we weren't just going to sign custody back to him and his girlfriend until they fulfilled all the court-mandated therapies and trainings, he punched a hole in the side of our house.

"You tricked us! You lied to us!" he screamed, "I hate you!" Riley had been in my life for ten years, and I had helped him with many challenging issues throughout his short and traumatic life. When he screamed, "I hate you!" it cut like a knife in my heart. I knew we were doing the right thing by keeping our grandson safe and doing what we could to make sure he grew up happy and healthy, but doing the right thing doesn't always feel good.

CHAPTER 33
D'andre Runs Away

I favored D'andre, and that became a problem. While I had loved Noah too little, I loved D'andre too much to the point I spoiled him and didn't hold him accountable. D'andre had given my own suffering, meaning when he had come to our home six years earlier, I realized that everything I had gone through could be used for some good. I could be a parent for kids with extreme trauma. I believed that kids like this needed a parent who could completely empathize and understand what they had gone through. Of course, I also had poor boundaries and a bit of a "save the world" complex, so when D'andre would act up, I would make excuses for him. This ended up not being so good.

D'andre didn't do well in school and had a lot of behavior problems. He had attended a behavioral school for emotionally disturbed children through the eighth grade and then transitioned to our local high school. He had a BMX bike and a skateboard, so he spent a lot of time riding around our town when he was younger. Being a Black family in a mostly White town, we bonded with the few other Black families.

One afternoon, a friend of Joseph's texted him a picture. "Hey, can you believe one of our people would do something so stupid?" She had texted a picture of a young Black boy lying in the middle of a street with a piece of plywood on his chest and another kid riding his bike over the plywood like a jump.

"Girl, that is my boy!" replied Joseph. And it was true. Joseph's friend didn't recognize our son repeating some challenge he had seen on social media, lying in the middle of a street with a piece of plywood on his chest. This epitomized our son, D'andre.

While Noah had chosen me to be the target of his disdain, D'andre had chosen Joseph. The first major meltdown that D'andre had was precipitated by him believing that Joseph was his biological father, who had done untold damage to this boy's soul. D'andre targeted Joseph when he got angry and wanted to get his way with something. I tried to be the peacekeeper with D'andre, but this was actually part of the problem. On at least three different occasions, I found D'andre had taken a knife and started pacing around Joseph. D'andre would glare at Joseph as he clenched the knife in his hand so hard his knuckles turned white. Each time I had distracted D'andre and redirected his anger toward something else.

There was also a lot of tension between D'andre and our other children. D'andre had been physically abusive to the twins and his sisters when he was younger. No one had forgotten that. He would get angry and hit and choke his siblings. During this time, he had also tried to touch our twins inappropriately in a sexual way. I don't remember this completely, but I didn't handle it well. I minimized it and tried not believing this could happen with our children. Joseph dealt with this incident better.

The twins resented me for this, and I didn't blame them. Any issues that had a sexual nature made me uncomfortable. Later, when D'andre was in the eleventh grade, he sexually propositioned his brother, Noah, through texting. This I handled even worse. Noah was livid, ranting and screaming through the house. I wasn't familiar with emojis and their meanings, but according to Noah, D'andre had sexually propositioned him. I again tried to minimize it and not bring attention to it. Any topic that was sexual in nature that involved our children deeply bothered me, so I tried to avoid it at all cost. Noah hated me for many things, but he especially hated me for how I handled *this* situation.

While D'andre was deeply damaged, he was also skilled at getting his way. When D'andre got his driver's license, he wanted a car. Not just any car, a Honda Civic SE with a stick. When I put my foot down and said no, he spun into such a depressed episode that

I had to bring him to a psychiatric facility. He wouldn't talk or stop crying for several days. He feigned not being able to walk and he stopped eating. When I brought him to the psychiatric facility, I used a wheelchair. I knew that emotional pain can cause a lot of physical manifestations. Both D'andre and Kareela had many physical manifestations of emotional pain.

While Joseph thought I was stupid for carrying D'andre and pushing him around in a wheelchair, I thought it was the right thing to do at the time. I did baby D'andre too much. I ended up getting him the car he wanted. Looking back, it was a huge mistake. At the time, I thought it was the right thing to do. Maybe it wasn't the right thing to do but the *easiest* thing to do. Getting him the car that he wanted was easier than telling him no.

D'andre was now a senior in high school and had turned eighteen. I was on a trip for work when D'andre called me. D'andre was loud and speaking quickly. "Papá kicked me out! He was mad crazy, yo!" He used strings of profanity-laden expressions to try to explain to me what had happened. I wasn't going to be home for a few more days, and there was nothing I could do. When I got home, Joseph gave me all the details. D'andre had puffed his chest up one night, wanting something that he couldn't have. D'andre then said he wanted to fight Joseph. Joseph was never afraid of taking a punch from any of our kids and told him to meet him outside. D'andre backed down and went to a friend's house.

D'andre was taken in by different friends but would ultimately get kicked out from fighting or hurting someone in the house. D'andre had anger issues and so much more. Joseph believed that I infantilized our son and made him dependent on me, leading to D'andre not doing anything for himself. Maybe I did. While I loved Noah too little, I loved D'andre too much and was afraid the day would come when he would no longer need me.

CHAPTER 34
Not My Daughter

One of my biggest regrets is that we had to spend so much time and energy dealing with the fallout of the abuse and neglect the kids experienced as young children that we didn't get to do the normal things a parent would do with their kids. Many of the things a person would learn or do as a kid had to be pushed to the side so we could deal with behavior issues and things we never even thought about before. Joseph and I tried to do many of the "normal" family things, but I think we gave up at some point.

Our daughter Kareela was extremely talented in many areas. She did well in school and was very artistic, athletic, and fun to be around. She was especially gifted in music and gymnastics. Everyone likes to think their kids are good at something, but Kareela genuinely had multiple gifts. She readily took to gymnastics. She was short, muscular, flexible, and had control over her body movements. She was also naturally gifted in music, particularly with stringed instruments.

Kareela had asked to learn to play the violin for a year and a half before we finally let her. We started in the summer when she was twelve. We found a violin teacher in our town who had been classically trained in Russia. Mr. Litvinov came to our home each week to give Kareela a violin lesson. Within a few weeks, Kareela was playing music we could recognize. Her teacher told us that she was the most naturally gifted student he had ever seen. Kareela started the school year with orchestra, which met right before the rest of school started. All of our kids walked to school, so Kareela left forty-five minutes early to get to orchestra three days a week.

We had started Kareela in a local gymnastics course, and she had done so well that we were also able to move her into a prestigious gymnastics academy where former students had gone on to participate in the Olympics. Kareela was a naturally talented athlete, and six hours a week, she was learning gymnastic basics and progressing nicely.

Music and sports are normal things that many kids participate in every day. A few months into the school year, Kareela's orchestra teacher called us to ask why she wasn't showing up for orchestra class before school. This was a surprise as Kareela left for school every day 45 minutes before the other kids to make it to orchestra. When we asked Kareela about missing class, she denied it. She claimed to be there and that the teacher just didn't see her.

Shortly after the call from Kareela's orchestra teacher, we got a call from her gymnastics school. Kareela had been accused of taking a girl's cell phone from the girl's locker. "Not my daughter!" is what I said, thinking that one of the few Black girls in the class was being accused of stealing and how unfair that was. "How do you know it was her?" I asked. They had looked online at the phone's location app to see that it was several blocks from our home. This was not conclusive evidence. "Anyone could have taken the phone," I said.

The next week, we got a call from Kareela's middle school. One of Kareela's friends had accused Kareela of taking her cell phone from her locker. The girls had shared their locker combinations with each other. A day later, we got another call from the gymnastics school. "Kareela has been caught on video going into another girl's locker and taking her cell phone," said the school's head coach. "We can't allow her to continue here."

Not my daughter. Not *my* daughter. What was going on? Kareela's grades had recently all turned into F's because she wasn't turning in classwork. She was skipping classes, and now she was stealing!

This was seriously crazy. I searched her room to find several phone cases, some of them personalized with other kids' names and pictures, and one cell phone. After talking with the middle school and gymnastics school, there were ten cell phones that Kareela was accused of taking over the last two months.

When we showed Kareela the evidence, she denied it and then finally said she did it "to make the other girls hurt like I did." We still had no idea where she had been when she hadn't been in orchestra.

While she was very talented, the trauma was coming out sideways and needed to be dealt with before any "normal" kid stuff could take place.

CHAPTER 35
The Perfect Family

At times, Joseph expressed that he felt that he had given up too much of himself to have the kids not be in a better state. We would see our friends' kids doing all the things many kids do: graduate from high school, go to college, or get married. Our friends' kids played sports, were in band, or had extracurricular activities. Joseph tutored our friends' kids in French, Spanish, and SAT prep. All their kids wanted to learn and tried hard. Their kids had focus and could push through when things got tough. Our friends' kids didn't run away, fail classes, get in fights, or get detention. Our friends never had to call the police or an ambulance to have their child taken to a psychiatric hospital. None of our friends were ever afraid that their kids would try to physically harm them.

I had been a parent to Vincent and Vance for six years before we adopted Stacey, Kareela, and D'andre. I had fun as a first-time parent. I loved and enjoyed all the things we did. They were a lot of work, but it was only physically exhausting. Vincent and Vance were three years old and didn't come with all the issues and trauma that came with our other kids. The work of raising our new kids was entirely different. It was emotionally and psychologically taxing. We never knew what to expect each day. Who was going to have a meltdown, or were we going to uncover some new horrible thing that happened to these kids? When we got Noah and Riley, there was more turmoil. Both of these boys were older and had many more years of trauma and distrust.

While I felt that no one could parent these children better than Joseph and I could, we were both exhausted. We had both put our own needs on hold for more than a decade. Sometimes I love my children, but I don't *like* them. Sometimes I hate my children; I'm not a perfect parent. They fight and argue with each other. Sometimes they gang up against each other, and sometimes they gang up against Joseph or me. They are extremely immature for their actual ages.

We aren't able to do the things normal families do, like go out in public together. Joseph and I have never been able to go out together and leave the kids at home. The few times we tried, the kids would get into some big fight, someone would run away, or someone would literally say they were going to kill themselves. Our family is not normal. There is nothing normal about these kids. Sometimes I am jealous of those people with naturally easy, well-behaved children.

All this being as it is, I love my children with all my heart. These are *my* children. Period. They don't look like me. I didn't raise any of them for their entire childhood. People have mistaken me for being their caseworker, their social worker, and their lawyer. They are *my* kids. I will fight to the death for them. My most favorite mistaken identity was a time at work when a coworker saw a picture of me with our first five kids sitting in a row on a bed. This was the first photo of all five, and I kept it on my work desk.

He looked at the picture and then looked at me. "Where were you a camp counselor?" he asked. In my head, I thought, *Are you joking? A camp counselor?* His expression looked benign and pleasant.

I looked at him unemotionally, straight in the eyes, and said, "That isn't a camp, that's my house. I'm their dad. These are my kids." I could see the mortifying embarrassment in his face.

I sometimes forget that I am a miracle and that my life is a miracle. My children's lives are miracles. I catch myself realizing this when I am doing the banalest of tasks. Like when I cook a grilled cheese sandwich for my youngest daughter, I find myself truly appreciating the smell of the frying butter, the melting American cheese, and the sound of the crackle and sizzle of the butter browning the bread. My daughter is bobbing her head to whatever music she has on her earbuds. Or I could be driving to work and see the rising morning sun in a perfect relationship with the cloud. The sun projects a pink and baby-blue cast on the bottoms of each cloud, and the glow of the sun rays shine behind the clouds like a halo. It truly is a hidden master-piece that is all mine. I appreciate these moments. Truly appreciate them. My life is a miracle. Every day is a miracle. *My children are all miracles.*

My life is by no means perfect. Our children's lives are not per-fect. My life is not easy, and I definitely do not have everything I want. However, I have everything I *need*. Everything. I have a family of my choosing and creation that I love and cherish more than I thought was possible. I love my children so much it makes me hurt sometimes. Raising my children gave my life meaning in a way I never realized. It is a miracle we all found each other.

CHAPTER 36
Who Am I?

It was now 2019, and twenty-five years had passed since I had to start my life over after losing my memories of growing up, going to school, and college. That resulted in losing my job, my home, my partner, and ultimately becoming disabled. I had learned basic facts about myself from my family and photos, and I had a few specific events that I remembered about my life pre-1995. I relearned my history from pictures and other people, but I truly didn't remember *who* I was. I had a long recovery from being handicapped and infantile, drug-addicted and mentally ill, and slowing redeveloping skills and abilities. I had become a father, a husband, and a grandfather. I had a career for almost twenty years with a big company and was fortunate enough to have traveled for work to many countries worldwide.

I had memories of the last twenty years, but I really didn't have more than superficial memories about who I was before April 1995. I know I was raised on a farm in Minnesota. I was sexually assaulted at thirteen. My family moved to Alaska when I was in the eleventh grade. I went to college and graduate school at the University of Alaska Fairbanks. I had two brothers and I worked at an aerospace company in Seattle after college. I met Stuart in college, and we eventually moved to Omaha, Nebraska, where I was in a car accident that left me handicapped with complete amnesia. That person I had been, who existed before the car accident, was gone. That person had died that warm spring day on US Interstate 80 in Omaha, Nebraska. Well…that's what I thought…

Before Thanksgiving break, when the twins were in tenth grade, I found myself staring at my reflection in the bathroom mirror. I was staring at a spiky, faux hawk haircut, a double chin, and wrinkles around my eyes. I truly didn't recognize myself. I don't mean this in a figurative way. I *really* didn't know who I was looking at. I saw this older version of me that I didn't recognize.

"Where did I get this stupid haircut?" I literally said out loud. "When and how did I get so fat?" I was flabbergasted at the person who was staring back at me. While you may have looked at yourself on occasion thinking the same thing, I had found that the twenty-seven-year-old me had woken up and come alive from nowhere. With little warning, the twenty-seven-year-old person who had been gone so long ago had literally come to life from a twenty-five-year long sleep. What the heck!

I had little warning that this was happening or going to happen, with the exception of two short incidents earlier in the week. Just a few days before, I had been driving to work and dialing through the stations on the radio. I had stopped on a country-western station without thinking and was singing along to the song on the radio. "I was just a country girl and saw you dancin' in the barn," I sang aloud melodically as if I knew these words and this melody.

I must have listened to the channel for about ten minutes, loudly singing along, before I said out loud, "I don't even like country music!" Still, there was something strangely familiar. This was my only obvious heads-up that something strange was on the horizon. The only other sign that something was different was our cat, Juliet. She came to me just a few days earlier and let me pet her. We had had this cat for six years, and I could never come close to her, much less pet her or pick her up. It was actually a family joke that the cat didn't like me. I was surprised, as I really had never been able to get close to this cat; now she wanted me to pick her up and play with her. She knew something was different. There may have been other signs, but I missed them.

As I stared at the stranger in the mirror, I literally saw flashes of sunlight as memories flooded in. I saw myself riding through the hayfields on our Minnesota farm, on my horse, Abigail, with the neighbor girls, who were my best friends, and their horses. This hadn't been part of who I was for the last twenty-five years. I remembered shoveling cow manure each morning before school and the smell of our chicken coup. I saw my Grandma Mary picking weeds in our large vegetable garden. She wore a large-brimmed straw hat and looked up to wave at me. "Hello, you're back!" My grandmother had died of cancer when I was fifteen, and I hadn't remembered her. I loved and missed her so very much at this moment.

I saw wagons of hay being pulled across the fields to a big red pole barn. All these things were gone for twenty-five years. I saw myself salmon-fishing with my parents for my birthday. We would go every year for my birthday on the Fourth of July, and we would build campfires with the lumps of bituminous coal that we would find along the sides of the river we fished in. I saw myself going to classes at college with my friends; I had an amazing group of friends. Awesome friends. I hadn't remembered them for twenty-five years. *This* was who I was—a son, a grandson, and a brother; a college graduate, a friend, and a boyfriend.

I had a boyfriend in college, my first true love. I could remember him. He came up to go to college in Alaska from Walls, Mississippi, and had Southern drawl. I saw my green AMC Hornet that I had in college. I would take road trips with my friends. I had friends. I saw Stuart and the parties we had at our home—big parties with lots of people and lots of friends. I knew so many people. This was the saddest memory to bear.

For the last twenty years, I always felt like I was missing something because I didn't have any long-term friendships. In actuality, I did have friends—a *lot* of friends. I just didn't remember them. These are the things that made me who I had been. I was so happy to feel and see all the memories as they came rolling in, but there was also loss and sadness that I hadn't remembered all these things for so long. I had lived an entire life before and I scarcely knew it. All these things were no longer part of my life. They were from a time past, from another life, *another* person's life.

I sat on the edge of the tub and let the memories flow in. So many things were lost. So many people were lost. So many good memories were lost. When I thought of my grandmother, I missed her. When I thought of my best friends across the road on our farm where I grew up, I missed them.

Long-term friendships had been something that I was robbed of. Everyone I knew now, I had known since I was thirty-ish. Not knowing how much I loved the neighbor girls and not understanding how important they were for me allowed me to let our friendships lapse for the last twenty-five years. Because I had moved across states, most of my friends from college had no idea where I was or that I had ever had an accident and lost all my memories.

I remembered my baby brother, Wayne, being born. I remembered taking him to do barn chores and all the things we did before he was thirteen years old. That's how old he was when I had my accident. I had many pictures of him, but I didn't have real memories of him before age seventeen or so. I did now. He was my first baby. I carried him everywhere I went. I did barn chores with him strapped to my back. Having my baby brother made me want to have my own kids one day.

I remembered college and the amazing group of friends I had made. I had very cursory memories of the people who existed in my life but not how I felt about them or what they meant to me. Again, because I didn't realize how much I loved them all or how important they were to me, I hadn't fostered those relationships over the last twenty-five years. None of them had known I was in a car accident. I had pictures and a basic understanding of who most of them were, but now I had actual memories with details of what we did and how I felt about everything. With my gain of memory came so much additional loss. Loss of the relationships I had had. Loss for the life I had and of all those opportunities. While I know there were other opportunities in the second life that I am grateful for, I still wondered what could have been for the first life.

Who would I have been if I was never hit by that truck? Would I have left Omaha? Would I have stayed with Stuart? Would I have ever adopted kids? Would I have adopted so *many* kids? Would I have gotten married? Would I have traveled the world? Would I have become an alcoholic, anyway? Would I have been successful at work? Would I have been happy? Would I? Would I? Would I?

More memories flowed in. Core beliefs, likes and dislikes, values, prejudices—so many things that make a personality had been taken from me. How could all of this have been erased?

I remembered my dad and grandpa. I loved them so much. Both of them had since passed, neither of them knowing that I had gotten better.

When I didn't know what I didn't know, I was okay. When I realized how much I lost, I was overwhelmed with loss and grief. The life I was learning about was gone and had been gone for a very long time, but I was now twenty-seven and fifty-two at the same time. Twenty-seven-year-old me not knowing that life was about to change forever and fifty-two-year-old me knowing the pain of loss, knowing what twenty-seven-year-old me had to go through and endure to get here to today. If I could go back in time to that morning in April 1995 when the blue truck ended my first life, would I tell myself to stay home? If I did stay home, I wouldn't suffer the pain of loss, amnesia, addiction, and disability. I also wouldn't have my children: Vincent, Vance, Riley, D'andre, Stacey, Kareela, and Noah.

Sitting on the edge of my bathtub was like sitting at the top of a hill and looking down on the life of someone I hardly knew. There were now two mes—the one before the accident and the one after. Both entirely different people from different backgrounds and walks of life. One grew up on a farm in Minnesota and then a small town in Alaska. The other grew up in urban Chicago. One listened to country music, and the other liked hip-hop. If these two people had met separately, they would never have been friends; they would have probably never even crossed paths.

CHAPTER 37
The Piano

My head and my heart were both overwhelmed. How could this be happening now? It had been twenty-five years since I was in a car accident that took my memories. I didn't truly know what I didn't know, who I was before 1995. I had been told things about my past and I had relearned things from other people, but I truly didn't remember them. For the most part, I had just remembered the things that people told me.

I had a piano and had always tinkered around with it. I always thought I was never really very good. I remembered how much I loved the piano and how I would spend hours practicing each day. I sat down at my dust-covered piano, opened a book, read the music, and began to play the music score. I played Beethoven and Greig. I could read music, and my fingers knew what to do. I had all these music books but was never sure why I had them. My hands hurt because they had not moved like this for twenty-five years, but the music was flowing along with the tears of joy. I *knew* how to play the piano. I *knew* how to play the piano. I knew I loved the piano, but I didn't think I knew how to play the piano very well. Memories flooded in. I *loved* to play the piano. It was my savior growing up. I practiced for two hours a day as a kid. I could express my emotions and release stress through playing. I loved to play the piano, and I still loved to play.

Memories came back from taking piano lessons as a child. I had taken piano lessons for ten years, starting from the age of six. I would go every Wednesday afternoon to Ms. Olsen's house. Ms. Olsen was in her fifties and lived with another older woman. She had two grand pianos in the front room of her house. I was afraid of her. She would tell me I was lazy and the worst student she ever had and didn't know why she wasted her time teaching me. I truly hated and feared her, but she was my only option if I wanted to take piano lessons. She was the only piano teacher in my small town in Minnesota. I would leave crying after every lesson but would not let my mom see that I had been crying. I would compose myself on the porch before leaving Ms. Olsen's house.

Looking back, she was extremely abusive, and I shouldn't have taken the abuse. I was sixteen years old when my family moved from Minnesota to Alaska, and I finally stopped taking piano lessons and abuse from Ms. Olsen. She told me until my last days with her how lazy and stupid I was. When I had graduated from college and graduate school, I had gone back to Minnesota to visit Grampa. I wanted to see Ms. Olsen and ask her why she was so mean to me for ten years, but she had died. She may have asked me why I kept coming back. My answer would have been that I would have endured anything to learn how to play the piano. Maybe Ms. Olson gave me the tenacity to endure what I had when I was brain-damaged. Push through no matter what because you want this. It doesn't matter what other people say. It doesn't matter what other people do. If you want this badly enough, you will endure whatever you need to accomplish your goal. When I thought this through, I had peace regarding Ms. Olson.

I knew I had played the piano. That was part of my past that was well documented. When I was learning to read and write two years after the accident, I also tried to relearn to play the piano. I had the music books from when I was a child. It was difficult, but I enjoyed the piano. The piano provided continuity of my past life with my current life.

Along with remembering how to play the piano, I also remembered going to college and my college education. For the last twenty years, I had gotten by with what I had learned on my own through books and practicing math with a pencil and notebook. I now remembered statistical concepts and math equations that I hadn't known for twenty-five years. I was able to do so much more at work as I now had the knowledge and life experiences of two separate people. For the last twenty years at work, I had struggled writing reports and decks, but I had known how to write well and loved it. I knew how to write well. I had the knowledge and skills of two different lifetimes' worth of learning. How could this be? Why now? How did this happen? I had no idea that a whole life was hidden behind a door in my mind, waiting for someone to open it and find that other world.

CHAPTER 38
First-Me and Second-Me

I now had two people living in my head who had each lived their own lives, had their own likes and preferences, and had their own core beliefs. I referred to the two people in my head as First-Me, the precar accident twenty-seven-year-old, and Second-Me, the fifty-two-year-old who lived after the car accident. Neither one had ever met before. When I lost my memory in 1995, I lost almost everything. Everything after that was learned from a mostly clean slate. When I learned to read again, I actually learned to read. I didn't remember how to read. When I learned math again, I didn't remember how to do math. I actually learned math for the first time. I never knew this about myself. I thought I was actually remembering how to do things over my years of recovery. It took months for me to process all the changes, to process all the new knowledge and learning that was unlocked.

The first thing First-Me did was make us lose forty pounds, get new clothes, and change our haircut. First-Me was vainer than Second-Me. It may have been that First-Me was still just twenty-seven years old, and younger people tend to care more about their looks than older people. It could also be that First-Me was simply vainer. We, I, lost forty pounds in the first three months of First-Me waking up. Second-Me always wanted to lose weight but couldn't. First-Me had the discipline that Second-Me never had. I had always had a full head of hair. I was blonde, but I regularly colored it to make it less ash and more golden blond. Second-Me loved hair coloring. First-Me thought it was stupid. First-Me won that battle. We stopped coloring our hair and changed the 1990s faux hawk to a more stylish asymmetrical look with long bangs and shaved sides. First-Me discovered online shopping, fell in love with it, and got new glasses, jeans, shirts, sweaters, and shoes. Second-Me hated shopping, both online and in a store.

In the first few months, I felt that First-Me was taking over the life that Second-Me had built, and I didn't like it. First-Me and Second-Me fought constantly about what was right and not right, what was the right thing to do or say. First-Me was much stricter with the kids, especially Vance and D'andre. First-Me couldn't understand why Second-Me let the boys get away with so much bad behavior.

The first time I realized that I was, we were, attracted to a White guy, I was shocked and surprised. For the last twenty years, I wasn't really physically attracted to White men, but First-Me was attracted to White men, almost exclusively. Second-Me was attracted to a wide variety of types of men, but Black men were at the top of the list. How had this rift happened? First-Me had beliefs and thoughts that Second-Me found extremely racist. Not KKK racist, but definitely everyday White-privilege racist. First-Me would have had no problem intimidating someone who was not White if it was in First-Me's self-interest to do so. Second-Me identified more with Black people than with White people. Second-Me had been "raised" in Chicago with a mostly Black family that Second-Me had created.

First-Me did not know Joseph or our children. Second-Me literally had to introduce First-Me to our children and to our husband, Joseph. Second-Me had to give First-Me the literal history of adopting our children and getting married. First-Me had to process all this new information and integrate the concept of Joseph and the kids with First-Me's values and core beliefs. There was twenty-five years of information to process! First-Me was single and childless. Second-Me was married with a large family. Second-Me also had a lot to process. I had had to relearn how to read and write after the accident. I had also relearned how to cook, work, and have relationships from a blank slate. The kids liked First-Me's cooking better than Second-Me's. Apparently, First-Me was a much better cook.

At work, I never liked writing presentation decks I wasn't good at. First-Me *was* good at it and liked doing it. First-Me was also more ambitious than Second-Me. First-Me made us get a different position at work that had more upward mobility. I started a new position at work six months after First-Me woke up. I hadn't ever initiated a new job move at work since getting hired twenty years earlier. Second-Me always went with the flow and accepted positions and moves that were offered. First-Me was much more assertive and self-confident than Second-Me.

I want to stop here for a moment. When this was happening, I had told Joseph about the day that twenty-seven-year-old me had woken up and remembered my life before 1995. Joseph was surprised but could tell something was different, something was off. He joked that it would be funny if I had now remembered that I was straight with a wife and kids somewhere. *That* would not have been funny. One of the few things that was the same with both First-Me and Second-Me was that they, we, were both gay.

I did not know what to tell my family about the conflict that First-Me and Second-Me were having. Who would believe it? First-Me would stare at Joseph and the kids suspiciously. First-Me was somewhat uncomfortable with Black people in general, probably from lack of exposure or general lack of knowledge. My family, growing up in Minnesota and then Alaska, regularly made racist jokes and references. I never challenged that growing up and didn't give it a second thought. I don't know that I would have ever thought of any of that as racist. I specifically remembered times when I was young, and my family would go off-road hunting on the Alaskan tundra. The tundra has large expanses of sphagnum moss that form mounds, apparently resembling afros. My family would refer to the tundra as n—— heads. As a child, at that time, I thought nothing of it. Second-Me was more than appalled.

I had conversations with myself for months.

> FIRST-ME. Joseph is your husband, our husband? Joseph is Black, right? He's kind of light-skinned. Is he part White or Hispanic or something?
> SECOND-ME. Are you implying that if Joseph was at least part White, this may be better than if he was all Black? Joseph is Black. Black people come in a wide range of shades because that's how genetics work.

Then First-Me had a fascination with Joseph's hair.

FIRST-ME. I want to touch Joseph's hair. I don't know why but I want to touch his hair. I have to touch his hair. Do you think he will let me touch his hair?

SECOND-ME. You are, we are, married to him. I don't think he'll think anything of you touching his hair. Touch it. You're being really weird about this.

First-Me really had a hard time with the kids.

FIRST-ME. Your kids don't look like you.

SECOND-ME. *Our* kids may not look like me, but they act like me. They have my mannerisms. They have my values. Kareela is my, our, virtual twin.

FIRST-ME. Why did you get so many kids? They can be ungrateful, rude, and obnoxious. You know they don't love you. They're just using you. You have to watch out for the big kid. I don't think you should trust him.

SECOND-ME. Sometimes I wonder why and how we adopted so many kids too.

The biggest conflict between First-Me and Second-Me was that First-Me was suspicious of our children. First-Me knew maybe two Black people ever and would never have dated a Black person, much less marry one. Did that make First-Me racist? First-Me kept tripping us up by overreacting when the kids would do something. First-Me was suspicious of the motives of our children and afraid they would steal or lash out. I kept having complete "what the heck" moments as Second-Me realized and judged First-Me for having such White-privilege thoughts. First-Me would then judge Second-Me for being naïve, so liberal, and such a doormat. Was I really this racist growing up? First-Me was also completely floored by how Second-Me let the children talk to us.

FIRST-ME. Did Vance just tell you to shut up?!

SECOND-ME. Vance was joking.

FIRST-ME. No, he wasn't. Why aren't these kids better behaved and doing more around the house?

Second-Me. I try but I can't make them do everything I would like them to do. There is a lot of history with trauma and mental illness and such.

First-Me. Uhhh, I don't care.

First-Me had been in full command for several days when we, I, considered the fact that leaving the kids and Joseph was an option. These were the most ungrateful kids ever. Joseph had told me on several occasions that Brown people should raise Brown children, and while that made me angry, I was beginning to see his point. What ties did I even have with them, anyway? First-Me had just met the kids, hadn't bonded with them, and didn't really want to.

Some days when I would wake up, First-Me was leading the day. Other days, Second-Me was leading the day. Some days both First-Me and Second-Me were chiming in throughout the day. First-Me had been leading for a few days when Kareela and Vance really pushed First-Me over the edge. Second-Me was more empathetic, too empathetic, according to both Joseph and First-Me. Second-Me empathized with the kids and the trauma they had experienced. First-Me was pissed off with the kids' bad behavior and worse attitudes. First-Me wanted to get away from all the drama and bad attitudes and find a new boyfriend and a new life. While Second-Me was happily married with children, First-Me was single, childless, and extremely stressed at the situation that we found ourselves in.

First-Me would say things like, "I don't even want to be married, and I'm definitely not ready to have kids. How in the world did I end up with so many kids? And not just any kids, kids with problems. Hard to deal with problems. And I don't think Joseph really loves you, us. He spends no time with me, us. He is critical of frigging everything I, we, say and do."

Second-Me would respond, "Well, you are, we are, married and we do have kids. Deal with it. These kids need me, us. These kids were sent to us for a reason. No one else could have raised them or even would have wanted to. You're right, they have problems—more problems than most kids. And kids need time and attention, so yes,

Joseph is not spending a lot of time with you, us. And you are kind of a dick, so there's that."

Kareela had begun acting out more than usual. Joseph and I had taken away her cell phone as a punishment, and she was going to make sure we felt as bad as she did. This round of bad behavior started with Kareela receiving a video call that Joseph accidentally answered while picking up her phone. The video call was a group chat from a group of teenaged boys who started cursing at Joseph. Why would Kareela get any calls from boys like this? Trying to question Kareela about this escalated into extreme bad behavior, and we decided it was better to just take her phone away. Kareela moped around the house for a few days, talking about how unfair we were and that we were too strict and no one else's parents would do this. This escalated to Kareela taking a butcher knife and stabbing holes in her walls, flatscreen TV, and smashing everything breakable in her room on the floor. She was in a rage and she was not able to turn it around.

First-Me could not comprehend a child acting like this and did not want to have to deal with it. Kareela was so out of control that I had to bring her to a psychiatric hospital's emergency room. This was too much for any parent to manage.

Vance had also been a disaster. He was failing every class because he just didn't want to do his homework. He was always angry and literally said mean things with an angry attitude 90 percent of the time he spoke. Even when he wasn't speaking, he was rolling his eyes or slamming doors. This was all too much. How did the kids' behavior get so unmanageable?

First-Me wanted to get the heck away from these kids with bad attitudes and behavior problems. They weren't First-Me's kids. The best solution would be to move far away, get a new job, and start over someplace else. And that is what First-Me planned to do. First-Me had lived in Seattle and loved it there. Seattle was all the way across the country from these kids and this life I found myself in. "This is not my life," First-Me would defiantly state. "I don't even want this life, these kids, or this husband!"

There were many jobs in Seattle, and First-Me believed that there were probably still friends there from more than twenty-six years earlier when First-Me lived there. For First-Me, Seattle was a recent memory. First-Me had a lot of good memories of living in Seattle. First-Me loved the mountains, the ocean, and the mild weather. First-Me loved going clubbing with friends and going to restaurants and day trips around the Puget Sound area. Stuart and First-Me had a beautiful house with a rose garden and a yard with a pear tree. I had Stuart in my life then. I didn't have Stuart any longer. I hadn't had Stuart in my life for more than twenty years.

Who am I?

CHAPTER 39
First-Me

Before I was a traumatized teenager, I was a happy and compassionate child. I led a somewhat idyllic country childhood. I was born and raised on a small farm in Northern Minnesota with cows, horses, and chickens. I loved living on a farm. I especially loved the animals and taking care of them. Each spring, purple martins would build mud nests under the outside eaves of our red barn, and barn swallows would build straw nests just inside the eaves on the inside of the barn. Cowbirds would lay their eggs in unsuspecting purple martin and barn swallow nests. Cowbirds don't raise their own babies. They lay their eggs in the nest of other birds. Cowbirds hatch first and then push out the eggs and newly hatched chicks of the purple martin or the barn swallow.

For a few weeks each year, when I would go into the barn as a child, I would find chicks and eggs that had been pushed out of their nests—purple martin chicks on the ground outside and barn swallow chicks on the cement floor inside the barn. My earliest memories of seeing the babies peeping on the floor was when I was four years old. I found a shoebox, put some hay in the bottom of the box, and built a nest for the babies. I would find a couple of baby birds every couple of days that needed to be rescued. Each year, I would find a dozen or so baby birds that were still alive. I would try to feed them chopped-up worms. They would never live for more than a couple of days, but each year, I would go through my ritual of finding a shoebox, building a nest, and then trying to feed the baby birds.

When I was ten, I finally saved one baby bird that lived. I raised one barn swallow from a hatchling on the concrete floor to adulthood. I was sad when I would find the chicks dead in my shoebox each year, and I would bury them in my mother's flower garden. It was important to me to give each chick a chance to thrive. Do what I could. This was apparently something that was innate in me as a child and now as an adult.

As I reflected on the person who had woken up after so long, I began to remember and process all these new "memories." I remembered that First-Me was clinically depressed and had taken antidepressants for much of my young-adult life before my accident. I never was really treated for the PTSD from being raped as a young teenager. I had been sexually assaulted again in college at nineteen when I was roofied at a dinner party with "friends." I couldn't move but could hear and feel everything. It was a horrifying experience.

After I was raped at nineteen, I told my best friend at the time that I had been raped. He laughed and said, "You can't rape the willing." I never talked to him after that. I didn't tell anyone else. Having no one understand what happened to you or what you went through is often worse than the experience itself. It is unfortunate that just a few hours or even a few minutes of something so violating can have such a negative impact on the entire rest of your existence, but it does.

First-Me had had severe anorexia and bulimia growing up and had been in an eating disorders support group through college and graduate school. First-Me had seen a therapist off and on for depression and anxiety. The anorexia and depression started after being raped and assaulted at thirteen. When I was a senior in high school, my anorexia was so extreme that I developed a form of hepatitis called starvation hepatitis. The white part of my eyes was yellow, and I weighed maybe 111 pounds. This was the same condition that I had seen in my son Riley when he was fourteen years old when his skin was gray and his eyes were yellow. My mother had taken me to the doctor several times, but no one ever asked me about eating or being abused. I had suffered in silence until my car accident at twenty-seven. Even at twenty-seven years old, I only weighed 125 pounds at five feet and ten inches. This was extremely thin. I would look at myself in the mirror and be disgusted with how fat I was. Through graduate school, I would binge Cheetos and corn chips before every test and then throw up in the bathroom in my dorm. My friends knew that I was bulimic and tried to get me to stop.

First-Me also knew something that gave Second-Me some peace. I was transported back to the day I was raped and beaten, a child of thirteen. I did walk home, and my mother did tell me not to tell anyone what had happened. However, I hadn't listened to her and I had called the police and reported the crime. We lived in a small rural town, and it was 1981. No police officer came, and I don't know if anyone ever went to see if the two little boys were okay.

I called the police in our small town every year on the anniversary of the rape to remind the police that our neighbor, the fat postmaster, was a pedophile and that I would testify if anyone else pressed charges. I called every year. I called after moving to Alaska, after graduating from college, and every year up until the year I was in a car accident that led to amnesia. It gave me some solace to know that I had tried to do the right thing by those boys. For twenty-five years, I had thought I walked away and never looked back. Walking away that night I was raped at thirteen was my biggest regret, but I hadn't just walked away. I tried to get help; help just never arrived. My need to make things right led me to adopt Vincent and Vance—the best thing I ever did in my entire life.

It took me months to process all the new information about who I had been with who I was now. I was sad for the loss, but I was happy to finally remember my past. I was stressed by the two very different people fighting for control in my head.

CHAPTER 40
Not Good Enough

Parenting as two different people was challenging. First-Me didn't really want to engage with the children and would check out. Second-Me was dedicated to raising the children. I had gotten a call from the principal of the high school telling me that both Vincent and Vance were going to have a Saturday detention. The twins had only started high school a month earlier, and I needed to ensure that they both showed up at ten o'clock in the morning, and they would have to stay until two in the afternoon. Both First-Me and Second-Me were pissed. Saturday detention was reserved for the worst infractions. D'andre had had Saturday detentions on multiple occasions over the last two years, but Vincent and Vance had not. D'andre had regularly had behavior issues, and it was not a surprise that he would get detentions. Vincent and Vance didn't have any behavior issues at school, and I was very angry and going to make sure this was the last detention they received.

Both boys had gotten a Saturday detention for different incidences. Vance had talked back to a teacher in his science class, and Vincent had been stopped in the hall when he was supposed to be in the lunchroom. Vance claimed that other kids said worse things and didn't get any detention, much less Saturday detention. Vincent claimed to be with two of his friends who didn't get any detention. The other boys were both told to go back to the lunchroom. I wasn't believing anything they said. Both First-Me and Second-Me did agree that whatever bad behavior had happened, it needed to stop.

Saturday morning was a bright and sunny day. Having to spend detention inside on a Saturday was bad enough. Having to sit inside on a day with good weather was worse. *Good enough for them*, I thought. I wanted to make sure that the boys didn't sneak out of doing detention like D'andre had done before. So when we got to the detention room, I ushered the boys inside and then waited outside the door until the teacher who would be monitoring the detention arrived. We were the first ones there. I was going to make sure they got the full punishment.

The first kid who arrived was one of Vincent's friends, a Hispanic boy in his grade. The next two kids who arrived had been on a basketball team with D'andre, both Black. I thought it was a weird coincidence that I knew the first three additional kids who had to do Saturday detention. I wondered why the kids that my kids were friends with had to do Saturday detention. Over the next few minutes, the Saturday detention room filled up with Black and Brown boys, most of whom I didn't know. Our kids' high school had about 1,500 students and was mostly White. At most, one out of four kids in the high school weren't White.

I was in a bit of disbelief when the detention teacher arrived. "You can pick your kids up at two," she said.

As I walked back to the parking lot and got in my minivan, I was angry and bothered. I turned the key and drove out of the parking lot. "Why were all the kids in Saturday detention Black and Brown boys like my kids?" I said out loud. First-Me was struggling to make sense of this.

> FIRST-ME. We know some of those kids, and they are trouble. D'andre was in Saturday detention several times.
>
> SECOND-ME. This is straight-up racist. There is no way that only Black and Brown boys get Saturday detention. There aren't even that many Black and Brown boys in our school.
>
> FIRST-ME. Our town can't be racist? Our school can't be racist? How can our kids' school be racist?
>
> SECOND-ME. It only takes one racist and a lot of other people to look the other way.
>
> FIRST-ME. Our kids, my kids, are not staying in that detention!

I turned around in the middle of the street and drove back to the school. First-Me was much more assertive than Second-Me. I walked faster than I had ever walked. Our kids, my kids, were 100 percent being victimized by racism right now, and First-Me could see it as well as Second-Me. This was *not* going to happen.

With First-Me in charge, I walked into the detention room. All the boys were sitting with their heads on their desks. They weren't allowed to read anything or do anything other than contemplate their punishment.

"Vincent and Vance, get up and go to the car!" I ordered. "I am sorry," I continued and looked at the detention monitor. "This is straight-up racist. There is no way my children are ever going to attend a Saturday detention. I will call right, right and wrong, wrong," I said very quickly and nervously. "This is wrong!" I stomped back to the car, and that was that.

First-Me pondered whether or not the thoughts and actions of our past were racist. I thought about this for some time, as this was among the most different aspects between First-Me and Second-Me. It was the most glaring difference between the two mes. We, I, agreed that it didn't actually matter if I didn't think I was racist or not growing up. It was not good enough to just not be a racist. You can't just turn a blind eye and allow racism to occur and watch other people do discriminatory things and not say or do anything. First-Me, like Second-Me, came to believe that you had to actively fight against racism. Simply not being racist was not good enough.

Everyone in our school had to know that only Black and Brown boys got Saturday detention. I'm sure none of them thought of themselves as racist, yet still, only Black and Brown boys got Saturday detention. The teachers had to know. The principals had to know, and all the Black and Brown boys had to know. The detention monitors *definitely* knew. How did so many people allow something so racist to persist without doing something to stop it?

CHAPTER 41
Kareela the Terrible and First-Me

Kareela was now fifteen years old and had been having more and more issues with depression, anger, and rage. She was dealing with all the normal things a teenaged girl had to deal with in addition to continuing to deal with the trauma that put her and her siblings into foster care and ultimately to be adopted. She struggled with maintaining friends and staying motivated to keep her grades up in school. She would go through phases of not taking care of herself and binge-eating. Except for a few rare instances, Kareela would never talk about what happened when she was five and six years old at her biological parents' home. Even during those times, she didn't disclose much of what happened. All of her therapists said that she was a closed book. Maybe she couldn't remember, maybe she didn't want to remember, or maybe it was just too difficult to think about, much less to talk about. Even though she didn't talk about the trauma she experienced as a child, her emotional pain was regularly being expressed in her behavior and actions.

It had only been six months since my memory came back of who I had been before the car accident. There was still a very clear distinction between the two people I had in my head. The two personalities were integrating all the facts of the two lives, but there were still significant differences, primarily regarding the children. First-Me was not as patient and understanding as Second-Me was with any of the children's trauma-related issues. In fact, First-Me was actually quite intolerant, and Kareela could tell that I wasn't the same person I had been over the last eight years.

With both First-Me and Second-Me chiming in, I was quite inconsistent with how I related to the children. Up until now, Second-Me would usually take the time to sit with Kareela and talk with her about how she was doing and how she was feeling. I would try to give her ideas for managing her depression and other emotional issues that I had learned to use over the last twenty years of dealing with my own mental illness. Kareela desperately wanted other people to make her feel better. Second-Me tried to make her feel better, but First-Me had little patience or desire.

Kareela had been back and forth in the psychiatric hospital several times over the last few months. She had only been home for three days this time when she had another extreme meltdown at home.

When Kareela was agitated, she would start by following me around our home and making provoking statements. She craved attention and wanted to make sure everyone knew she wasn't feeling right. "I'm going to run away from home so you can never find me," she stated defiantly. "I'll let anyone take me home so I don't have to ever come back here."

First-Me was in control this day and wasn't particularly interested in placating Kareela. "I will just call the police," I told her. This went on for more than six hours, Kareela following me around our home and yard, saying, "Tell me I can leave, tell me I can leave, tell me I can leave." She could literally repeat this for hours on end to try to get her way with whatever she wanted that moment.

First-Me found this behavior to be very unnecessary and was trying to ignore Kareela. This wasn't the reaction Kareela was used to and definitely not the reaction she wanted, so she started damaging things in our home. Her primary motive when she was spiraling out of control was to make other people hurt like she did. Her anger came out sideways; she poured gallons of water into our clothes dryer. With a large household, a washer and dryer were critical. She intentionally clogged sink drains. She broke random things around the house that were important to me. All this was exhausting. Kareela was hurting on the inside and was going to make sure everyone hurt like she did.

This was the first time that First-Me was primarily present and had to manage Kareela during a meltdown. Taking her to the ER at the psychiatric hospital was a risk, but there was nowhere else to go. There was no other help for Kareela. We couldn't leave her unattended when she got like this, and we couldn't go to sleep even though it was quite late at night. Kareela was a danger to herself and had drunk cleaning products in the past to get attention. She would also cut herself.

I had taken her to the emergency room several times in the last few months. Sometimes they would admit her, and sometimes they wouldn't. If they didn't, she would come home even more defiant and angry, which would result in another trip to the emergency room. Sometimes the second trip was within hours of returning home from the ER. Every time we went, we would have to sit waiting for up to eleven hours to see whether the admitting doctor would keep her there or not. More than half the time, they would send us home.

"She isn't going to kill herself right now, so she doesn't meet the criteria for hospitalization," is what we would hear.

"Are you kidding me?!" I would yell. "She has told me multiple times today that she is planning to kill herself."

"Well, she didn't tell me that, so she doesn't meet the criteria," is what the doctors would usually reply. I really hated the entire emergency room staff, and I could tell that they were tired of having us come and plead for help with Kareela. There are no systems set up to truly support families with extremely damaged kids. It felt more like hospitals and agencies were trying to protect themselves from having parents dump off kids with bad behavior that they didn't want to deal with as well as reduce any legal liability.

Regardless, Kareela was now completely spiraling out of control at this time, and First-Me knew that I had to take her to the hospital again. She was extremely vile and mean when she was having a breakdown. She turned into Kiki, some persona she came home with from one of her stays in a residential treatment center. Kiki was a mean girl who would fight and rebel against anything we wanted her to do. Kiki would lie and steal to get what she had wanted.

As Kiki, Kareela had parlayed a one-week stay in a mental hospital to six weeks when she told her doctor that we, her parents, beat and starve her and that she was too afraid to return home. When the switch flipped and she became Kiki, there was nothing we could do. She would need to stay in some psychiatric facility until she could return to the girl we knew. "I'm going to run away and let anyone pick me up, and you will never see me again!" she screamed. Kareela had tried to run away several times in the last few months, only to be found by the police. Joseph didn't drive, so I would take Kareela to the hospital myself while he took care of the rest of the kids.

First-Me got Kareela in our minivan.

"I know you hate me!" she screamed. "I want you to take me to my *real* family, not the hospital." She hadn't pulled the "real family" card in a while. "Take me to my grandma! Take me to my grandma!" she screamed repeatedly as she kicked the dash in our minivan and slammed her hands on the windows.

"You mean the real family that won't let you visit!?" I screamed back at her. Kareela's biological grandmother only lived ten minutes from our home but wouldn't allow the kids to visit. The grandmother claimed it was because her grandchildren were adopted by "the gays," but we knew that we had nothing to do with it. The entire biological family was damaged from trauma, drug abuse, and alcoholism. We believed that the guilt of allowing her grandchildren to be abused and then put up for adoption was the reason she wouldn't see them. The grandchildren were a reminder of the failure of her own unresolved traumas.

I had made the mistake of talking badly about Kareela's biological family in front of her before. No matter how horrible a biological family is, no kid wants to hear that from anyone else. There is some loyalty no matter how misplaced. I detested Kareela's biological family—her grandmother, her mother, and especially her father.

When you have an incredibly damaged child, you can get to a point where you become numb—numb to their crying and screaming, numb to their lying, numb to their threats, and numb to their pain. Becoming somewhat numb is necessary to manage the regular pain and anguish your child expresses without going mad yourself. You need to balance caring with being able to function and help your child. Anyone could see Kareela was hurting right now. We just didn't know what to do to make anything better for her.

"Kareela, it's eight thirty at night. Your grandmother is most likely asleep in bed!" I yelled back her. "Do I need to call the police to get you to calm down!?" I screamed this rhetorical question to get the focus off going to her grandmother's house. My voice hurt from verbally sparring with Kareela for the last several hours. We sat in the minivan for an hour with Kareela screaming and ranting about wanting to be brought to her grandmother's house.

"If you don't take me to my grandma's house, I am going to kill myself!" she screamed. "I have a knife hiding in my room, and you won't find it!"

Joseph and I had to call the police at least six times in the last few months to get help with Kareela. Either she was too angry and violent for us to manag, or she had run away from home, and we needed help finding her and bringing her back. The first time you have to call the police on your own child, you have crossed a line that you never thought you would have to cross.

"I want to kill myself. I want to die!" Kareela screamed and then slammed her fists on the window of our minivan as I drove toward the hospital. She stomped her feet on the dash and kicked the windshield. I was really hoping she would not break out the front window with her feet.

"Please, let's just make it to the hospital in one piece," I begged the universe.

"Kareela, why are you so angry!? Why are you so frigging mad?! Who are you mad at?!" First-Me yelled back at her, trying to get her to focus and to not lose my mind.

She paused, took a deep breath, and yelled, "Because… because…because… I…was…raped…by…my…father! There are you happy? I said it. I was raped by my father. I was raped by my father!" she yelled back.

I was shocked, and both of us suddenly became quiet and said nothing more. The silence was deafening. We both stared at each other as tears welled in her eyes and in mine. It was the first quiet moment we had all day. In the last seven years, Kareela had never ever told us what actually happened when her father would take her into her room by herself. She would have only been five or six years old. First-Me couldn't believe what we had just heard. First-Me was aware of the kids' traumas but hadn't actually been around to experience the ramifications. What a monstrous thing to endure. What a horrible secret to hold on to. My head began to hurt from pressure as tears slowly dripped from the corners of my eyes.

I broke the silence and asked very softly, "Kareela, why wouldn't you tell anyone until now?"

She sat quietly and then responded with a scrunched-up face and a frown. "Who wants to admit their father raped them?"

First-Me got it. Second-Me got it. *I* got it. Who would want to admit that?

CHAPTER 42
You Are My Daughter

When we arrived at the hospital, First-Me had to explain to the attending emergency room doctor what was happening with Kareela. First-Me had been in command for the day and was extremely stressed with having to deal with Kareela.

"Are you the father?" asked the doctor.

"Yes, I am Kareela's father," I said. Kareela's eyes were puffy, and she looked expressionless. She had on an oversized black sweatshirt and had the hood pulled mostly over her face. She would get this way when she was questioned by anyone about what she was feeling. She would go to some dark corner in her mind and hide. "I need to get my daughter help," I told the doctor.

I was exasperated at yelling and screaming with and at Kareela for the last few hours. My throat hurt from yelling, and my voice was hoarse. *My daughter*, I thought to myself, *is she really my daughter?*

We were assigned an examination room in the Emergency Department. Kareela lay on the gurney, and I sat in a chair, trying to position myself comfortably. It was painful for even a stranger to see the emotions Kareela was experiencing right now. First-Me was going to try to talk to Kareela. It was obvious she was hurting and needed comforting.

"Kareela," I said, "I know how you feel."

"No, you don't! No, you don't! How can you? Huh, how can you?" she stated emphatically. Her eyes were wide open as she stared at me with her mouth hanging open. We were both tired from screaming at each other for the last few hours, and it was very late at night.

"I do know how you feel," I said. I had said that too confidently. I had wondered if I was ready or able to tell Kareela my own story. The kids knew that I had a car accident and that I had recovered from amnesia. I still had the myoclonic ticks that made me twitch and bark on occasion. I had told the older kids that I was a recovering drug addict, but I hadn't told any of them about being sexually assaulted. It just didn't seem appropriate. Was Kareela ready to hear that her father had been sexually assaulted too? Was I ready to tell her that I had been sexually assaulted? I am her father, not her friend, not her therapist. Am I ready to have my kids know my whole story?

First-Me had been raped at thirteen years old. While this was one of the few things that Second-Me had also known, First-Me knew about living with the shame and horror of this event as a teenager on a farm in Minnesota and then as a young adult. Second-Me knew about the rape and that I was not supposed to tell anyone what happened, but that was about it. First-Me had suffered in silence for years with anorexia and bulimia, with shame and with guilt. First-Me was then sexually assaulted again in college. I told no one about that after being made fun of by a "friend."

I took a deep breath. "Kareela, you know, boys can get raped too." Kareela sat and stared at me in disbelief with a look of disdain. I kept going. "I do know how you feel…because when I was thirteen… I was raped by a neighbor man while I babysat his kids." Kareela looked at me with disbelief and discomfort. "And I was raped again in college, and I never told anyone." I looked at her at that moment to give me some comfort. "You are the first person I have ever told about being raped in college." We both sat in silence as we pondered the gravity of what we had both shared. I had said it. I got it out. I told my daughter that I, too, had survived a sexual assault. Boys can get raped too. She had told me, told someone, that she had been raped by her father.

The door had finally been opened, at least for right now. Kareela and I talked all night as we waited in the emergency room. Kareela had finally started talking. After eight years of saying virtually nothing of her abuse and her trauma, she finally began to talk. She recounted seeing her mother get hit with the aluminum bat; this was something that D'andre had also shared. She recounted going without food for days at a time and getting beaten by her father for spilling a bowl of ramen noodles. Kareela had always alluded to abuse, and it was obvious from her behavior over the last eight years that something really bad had happened, but she never really told anyone *what* had happened. She then told me about first being molested by her father and then later about being sexually assaulted. How could something so horrible be real?

My daughter, I thought to myself. *Kareela is my daughter.* It is my fifty-third birthday, the Fourth of July, a national holiday, and I am sitting in the emergency room with my daughter Kareela. It has now been more than twenty-six years since the day I was in a car accident on Interstate 80 in Omaha, Nebraska. The day that would end one life but start another. It is now two o'clock in the morning, and we have been sitting here in the emergencey room for four hours and will probably still be sitting here for several more.

The world works in mysterious ways, and right now, this night, I understand. Kareela is my daughter, not Second-Me's daughter, *my* daughter. As the children's story was investigated, Joseph and I were eventually told by Child Protective Services that Kareela and her siblings suffered some of the most extreme child abuse that their agency had ever seen. My daughter had experienced some of the worst abuse a child can endure. I had also endured some of the worst traumas anyone should have to endure. We were brought together by fate. I was meant to be her father, of this I am sure. I have never been more sure of anything.

CHAPTER 43
One Hundred Years

At the beginning of this story, I told you that there will be a few things in your life that will mark a "before the event" and "after the event" time. Some of these will be horrid, and some will be amazing. I have had some of both. I don't know if I would have had aspired to have the amazing things in my life without having to endure and overcome the horrible. Perhaps *you* can aspire for more amazing things in your life without having to endure anything terrible.

I don't know if you believe in God or Allah, Buddha or Ganesh, Mother Earth, or a Higher Power. That is not for me to judge and only for you to figure out on your journey through life. I do believe there is a God, and I asked God for a very long—why? Why did I get hit by a truck so many years ago? Why did I have to be crippled and morbidly depressed for so long? Why did I have to have amnesia? Why did I have to be sexually assaulted and physically abused? Why did I have to become addicted to drugs and alcohol? Why did I have to suffer the indignities of abject poverty? Why did I have to lose everything? Why did I have to suffer through so much pain? Why? As humans, we want to know *why* things happen when maybe this just isn't the right question to ask.

Accepting "what is" is critical to recovering from any tragedy. This is my circumstance. It happened. I cannot change the past. I cannot undo the past. You may never know why something happened. Even if there was a real answer to *why*, that answer may never be a good enough answer. Maybe the right question is, what can I do with this? What can I do now? Maybe this is a more important question than answering, "Why did this thing happen?" Bad stuff happens all the time. I had many years where my circumstances in life continued to get worse. Every time I thought they couldn't get worse, they did. I went from being crippled with amnesia to drug-addicted and mentally ill. There may be no answer to *why*. It just is.

Did I handle everything the right way with each kid in each situation? Absolutely not. Not even close. Did I try my best at the time with the knowledge and mental strength I had? Most of the time, was my intent for each child to be happy and successful adults? Yes, I can say unequivocally that my intent was always in their best interest. Did everything turn out as I would have liked? Sometimes, enough times.

I believe God had a larger plan for me, for Joseph, and for our children. Maybe not to have me get into a car accident where I became crippled and drug-addicted, but once I was, to bring me on a journey to where I learned and recovered enough so that the children I now have could have a parent. A parent who would love them through all the trauma, anger, bad decisions, and bad behavior. I believe that God sends messages. Sometimes we see them, and sometimes we don't. I believe God led me on this journey to recover from amnesia and addiction to gratitude and recovery.

I am by no means a perfect person or a perfect parent. I am seriously flawed. I have anger issues and self-esteem issues, and I blame others for stuff every day instead of taking responsibility for my part. I still make bad choices and am somewhat narcissistic. Joseph would say that I am *very* narcissistic. I swear like a sailor when I'm in the car and will occasionally act like an entitled asshole in public when things aren't going my way. But I try to be better all the time, and I keep trying no matter what.

I aspire to live to be one hundred years old. I hope to be around as long as I can to support my children on their own journeys. Each one of them needs me, and I need each one of them for as long as we can be in each other's lives. I lost my father when I was thirty, and I still need him today, many years later. My children will need Joseph and me no matter how old they get. We are their parents. I hope to have twenty grandchildren whom I can take to the park and pool and the arcade. I want to experience lots of birthday parties, holidays, and weddings.

I know my children will continue to struggle in life. Maybe more than most. My children didn't come into this world with things they needed—safety, love, trust, or joy. These deficits can leave a lasting impression on your soul. Life is not a straight line. It has many twists and turns. My children still struggle. *I* still struggle. That is the joy of life—struggling together as a family, making each other better people, being there for each other in joy and in sadness, in celebration and in mourning.

The key to my life has always been perseverance, and hope has been my fuel. I need to be there for my children as they grow up and become parents and grandparents. I need to be there to make sure the cycle of violence and abuse they were born into has ended. My life has purpose and meaning beyond what I ever thought possible. I want to teach my grandchildren and maybe my great-grandchildren perseverance. I want to teach them to plant a garden, to ride a horse, and to spin angora wool into yarn.

EPILOGUE

I have written a story for my children. We adopted some, fostered some, and just took in a few more along the way. I want you all to know how much I truly love you. My life would not have been complete without each one of you in my life. Not everyone is dealt a good hand in life. It is important to do something good with what you are given no matter what it is. The best lives don't come from getting everything easily. Getting everything for nothing grows discontent and dissatisfaction; entitlement can be debilitating.

When you have to work hard for what you have, it is truly appreciated. You understand what is actually important to you when you have to decide to work for something and make sacrifices to have that thing. I have lived my best life, a life I would not have known without experiencing the tragedy and trauma. I have had to work hard to recover from brain damage, amnesia, drug addiction, and mental illness. Because of this, I appreciate each day and I love each moment that I am given. I truly appreciate the people in my life; I appreciate each one of you. My road is not a road I would wish anyone to take. All of you, my children, have come into this life with things no one would wish to have imposed upon them. All of you must find your own way.

You must first acknowledge whatever bad thing that happened and forgive those who imposed it on you. You must then forgive yourself. You had *nothing* to do with the bad things that happened to you. You were a child. You must work hard to make things better. It may take you one hundred tries or more, but you must keep trying. I know that it is not fair, and you resent the fact that you have to work so hard to get to a place where others are starting from with no work. I know this. Do not let resentment become your own imposed trauma.

There will be monsters that will try to feed on your soul. Don't let them take what is good in you. Some of you have experienced unspeakable horrors at very young ages. Deal with those horrors. Don't let them take up more room in your head and steal more years of your life. Don't let them. If you live a hundred years, make sure the first ten don't rule or ruin the last ninety.

You are never too old to start over. I learned to walk again at twenty-nine. I learned to read again at thirty. Aspire to be better. You deserve it. Each one of you deserves a "best life." Happiness is a state of mind, as is unhappiness. You need to believe you deserve to be happy in order to *be* happy. Choose happiness over unhappiness. You are years away from your trauma and from your abuser. Choose happiness. Choose life. Choose your best life. I love you, my children, all of you. In your life, you will either get bitter or get better. It's that simple. You either take what has been dealt and allow it to make you a better person or allow it to tear you down. The choice does not belong to fate; it belongs to you.

ABOUT THE AUTHOR

Danny James and husband, Joseph, are raising their eight adopted children and their grandson in their forever home outside of New York City with their dog, several cats, and even more angora rabbits. Both are dedicated to raising their children and advocate for children in foster care to have the resources they need to grow up happy and healthy.

Because of an accident with complete amnesia at twenty-seven years old, Danny has lived two separate lives. The first life as a young White man who was raised in a rural environment on a farm in Minnesota and then a small town in Alaska. The second life started after Danny lost his memory in a car accident and became severely handicapped. In the second life, Danny started over in an urban environment in Chicago and was raised by his Black family that grew around him. He had no memory of his first life and identifies more with Black people than with White people.

CPSIA information can be obtained
at www.ICGtesting.com
Printed in the USA
LVHW050731030322
712397LV00003B/364